EIGHT MONTHS AT MOUNT SINAI

Eight Months at Mount Sinai

A Theologian Reflects from Death's Borderland

ERIC J. TITUS
Foreword by Kendra VanHouten
Afterword by Nancy Titus

RESOURCE *Publications* • Eugene, Oregon

EIGHT MONTHS AT MOUNT SINAI
A Theologian Reflects from Death's Borderland

Copyright © 2024 Eric J. Titus. All rights reserved. Except for brief quotations in critical publications or reviews, no part of this book may be reproduced in any manner without prior written permission from the publisher. Write: Permissions, Wipf and Stock Publishers, 199 W. 8th Ave., Suite 3, Eugene, OR 97401.

Resource Publications
An Imprint of Wipf and Stock Publishers
199 W. 8th Ave., Suite 3
Eugene, OR 97401

www.wipfandstock.com

PAPERBACK ISBN: 979-8-3852-1321-4
HARDCOVER ISBN: 979-8-3852-1322-1
EBOOK ISBN: 979-8-3852-1323-8

07/16/24

Scripture references unless otherwise noted are from the New Revised Standard Version © 1989

This book is dedicated to:
my family: Nancy, Samuel, Valerie, Penelope, and Jack, who are my inspiration,
Jackie Fenaroli, my living donor,
and my donor who remains unknown but lives with me every day.

There is no soundness in my flesh because of your indignation;
there is no health in my bones because of my sin.
For my iniquities have gone over my head;
they weigh like a burden too heavy for me.
My wounds grow foul and fester because of my foolishness;
I am utterly bowed down and prostrate;
all day long I go around mourning.
For my loins are filled with burning,
and there is no soundness in my flesh.
I am utterly spent and crushed;
I groan because of the tumult of my heart.
O Lord, all my longing is known to you;
my sighing is not hidden from you.
My heart throbs, my strength fails me;
as for the light of my eyes—it also has gone from me.

—Psalm 38:3-10—

Table of Contents

Foreword by Reverend Kendra VanHouten | ix

Acknowledgments | xiii

Introduction: Anticipation and Reality | xv

Prologue | 1

1. Jackie—My Living Donor | 3
2. Death Begets Life—My Deceased Donor | 8
3. Food Fights | 14
4. Delusions, Hallucinations, and Near-Death Experiences | 21
5. Nancy, My Rock Star | 31
6. Samuel, Valerie, Penelope, and Jack | 39
7. When Hope Unborn Had Died | 51
8. The Hospital Staff: Acts of Kindness (and Cruelty) | 59
9. The Community of Faith | 65
10. The Sound of Silence | 76
11. Mountain Men | 81
12. Crossroads | 88
13. Recovery and Recovering | 92
14. How am I Doing Today? | 97

Epilogue | 103

Afterword by Nancy Titus | 107

Appendix: Death and Dying | 113

Foreword

by Reverend Kendra VanHouten

It was December 31, 2019, when I received a text from one of Eric's children: "It would be really good if you could come today." Within the hour, I was making my way to the train station. It didn't occur to me until I was on the train from Poughkeepsie that I was headed into Manhattan on New Year's Eve. Thankful that my stop was distant enough from the partygoers, who I imagined were already gathering, ready to celebrate, I made my way to Mount Sinai Hospital, unsure of what I was walking into but confident there would be no party. For the next eleven weeks, until the pandemic put a stop to it, I would take the bus from Kingston to Manhattan nearly every Friday, ten to eleven short trips in total, a drop in the bucket to the journey Eric was on.

I met Eric in the spring of 2012 after the Titus family had returned from Croatia. Mutual friends and colleagues seemed to be making a big deal about this guy Eric who was back in the Hudson Valley, and they were so excited. I wondered what was so great about this guy, briefly introduced myself at a meeting, and moved on. If I'm honest, I probably overheard him talking with a couple of colleagues and friends and thought, "This guy's way too intelligent for me; we'll never be friends," and kept walking.

Little did I know that somewhere down the road we would become friends. He often called for contact information for mutual colleagues to the point where I would begin to answer calls from him with: "Directory assistance, how may I direct your call?" We would laugh, and then begin to check in and share how ministry and life were going.

As pastors, we are often invited into the sacred spaces of people's lives. Not only do we sit in the ashes, in the dark, broken spaces, but we are also invited to share in the joy-filled and life-giving moments. And for many ministers, no matter how much we love our calling (or say we do), as

Foreword

Ministers of Word and Sacrament, it also means that we often have a very small number of folks that we let in to share our own sacred and holy joys and sorrows with. Eric and Nancy are the opposite. Because of the authentic way they show up in the world, throughout their lives, they have a crowd of witnesses that span the globe, all of whom were busy praying and seeking updates during Eric's illness and recovery. It was and is a humbling honor to be in this space with Eric and Nancy and their family.

During the January visits, when Eric was at his most fragile state, I would text mutual friends and colleagues to ask what I should read to Eric (the very friends who were probably talking with Eric the first time we met). They responded with a list. Once at his bedside, I sat down, opened my Bible and readings on my phone, and started reading aloud. At one point, while I was reading, Eric got restless, as if to indicate that he didn't want to hear that. Ha! I giggled and promised I wouldn't tell our friends and moved on to reading the Psalms and Heidelberg Catechism Q&A 1: "What is my only comfort in life and in death? That I belong in body and soul, in life and in death to my faithful savior Jesus Christ."

I have sat with many dying people, some who have survived and are living their best life as they are able, and some who are no longer with us. The words *I belong*, the words of this assurance, have taken on a depth of beauty and meaning as there was often nothing we could do while we waited but live and be assured God was present even when the darkness we felt seemed to be hovering.

In mid-January, I made my way down to Mount Sinai to spend the day with Eric while Nancy was home for a much-needed break. Eric was in the Transplant Intensive Care Unit and was at one of his lowest points, maybe a week before his second transplant. The day was spent sitting next to his bed reading Scripture. Praying, reading, and trying not to cry, holding his hand so he knew someone was in the room with him. After some time, I stepped out for a break. Turning the corner toward the elevator, the piano in the atrium six floors below began playing Leonard Cohen's "Hallelujah." As the music played, the sun broke through the window into the building. I stood there and wept. Unsure if it was out of relief that there was hope on the horizon or fear that I would go back into the room and Eric's body would be lying there lifeless and empty. I think in that moment, it was holding the tension of both, yet profoundly thankful that even in the moment, Eric's spirit could hold the promise and knowledge that he belongs, in his living and in his dying—and dear God, please let him live!—that he belongs to the God who loves him and is with him each moment. After a few minutes, I regrouped and walked back into the room, returning to my chair, quietly reading and praying.

Prayer. I'm not sure I have ever prayed so much in my life than during those months my friend was in the hospital. Anne Lamott's book on prayer, *Help, Thanks, Wow*, would be my guide. There were days when all I could do was muster up the prayer: "Help my friend, Eric, God. Help my friend, Nancy. Please, don't let Eric die." And then to walk into his room and hear him whisper hello, brought a weepy prayer of "Thanks, God." When he was standing in the pulpit preaching at a worship service several months later, the prayer was simply, "Wow, God . . . Just wow!"

The book you hold in your hands is a story of one man making his way forward. Some might say making his way back, but as you will read, Eric is living into the full meaning of what it means to belong in this world and be transformed. Don't let Eric fool you into thinking that it's only (as if eight and a half months isn't enough time!) the time he was at Mount Sinai Hospital. In these pages you can see glimpses of his journey up the mountain, on the mountain, and tumbling down into the depths, down into valleys. The story Eric tells is messy; it's hard and painful. However, it is also real, honest, amazing, and painfully beautiful. As I read the following pages, I relived some of Eric's story and our visits, but I also found myself reflecting on my own life, my own dealings with my mortality, my own faith, and how I show up in life.

I've mentioned Eric and our friendship, but the truth is, I'm beyond grateful for each member of the Titus family, thankful they are in this world. They each show up to the table, bringing their gifts, their story, and their willingness to extend hospitality to welcome me into their lives. Nancy never missed the opportunity to inquire as to how I was doing, even as we were both absorbing and processing over lunch in the cafeteria what Eric's hand gestures meant that morning. Eric, Nancy, and their children have endured many traumas and challenges, but they continue to rise up, finding strength and laughter, hope and comfort, and above all—a deeper love.

As you read these pages, may you be amazed, moved to reflect, curious, and grateful to God for the way God shows up and sends reminders that you, too, belong.

Acknowledgments

There is no way, when relating a story about a razor's edge struggle between life and death and dying, to thank all the people who were involved in that struggle with me. This includes not only doctors and surgeons but also nurses, personal care assistants, people keeping rooms clean, people who prepared meals, pharmacists, lab technicians, volunteers, friends, and colleagues who came to sit, sing, and serve at my bedside. This was a massive ensemble, all a necessary part of my survival.

There's also no doubt that without my family and my community of faith I would not be here, most especially the churches of the Reverend Mid-Hudson Classis, and my past congregations, St. John's Reformed Church and Fishkill Reformed Church with special mention of my current congregation, Pultneyville Reformed Church. I also thank those churches that ministered to my wife as she lived her life between Red Hook and Manhattan, especially Elmendorf Reformed Church and Church of the Living Hope. The World Council of Churches even came alongside Nancy at one point. As I danced the tango on that razor's edge, I am quite convinced that both the medical sciences and the power of faith played their proper role in keeping me grounded in this life. Related to this are my colleagues who walked beside me: Fr. Masud Ibn Syedullah, Rev. Kendra VanHouten, Rev. Gloria McCanna, Fr. Patrick Buckley, Rev. Renee House, Rev. James Alley, Rev. Richard Otterness, and Rev. Doug Leonard. They all played particular roles during my odyssey. My friends Shari and Brian Juranic hung with me in uncounted ways. My friend, Jay Wright, was a regular visitor and played prominently in my time at the hospital and even in my hallucinations.

When one tries to name names, there is a danger that someone important will be left out. In my case, many will be left out for reasons of space and the human capacity for lapses in memory. Nevertheless, I will name a few people here. My immediate family: my wife Nancy, our children,

Acknowledgments

Samuel and his spouse Jack, Valerie, and Penelope gave so much. I love and honor each of them more than words can say. They are the beat of my heart, my *quod vivere*.

I must also with the deepest gratitude remember my living donor, my first donor, Jackie Fenaroli, her husband Pete, and their children, Gianna and Matthew. Jackie's donation, as you will find, was lifesaving and got me into the transplant process, giving me time that I needed to wait on organs from a deceased donor. Without her kind and selfless gift, I might have died even before being admitted to the hospital. My life is owed to her, a thing which cannot be repaid.

My deceased donor, who is with me each day, is the one to whom I give special acknowledgment during the course of each day. How does one begin to grapple with gratitude for such a thing? I try most days to remain positive but on many days I find this extremely difficult. I try to find a reason and purpose that exceeds the cost, but there is none, at least none that someone else might also have achieved without such cost. Still being present with family, the very gift of which he was deprived, is my ever-present reason above all reason to be grateful and alive. I have been given by this person a gift which most of us take for granted every single day—time.

To my surgeon Dr. Sander Florman, and his residents, interns, nurses, attendants, and techs; my hepatologist, Dr. Joseph Odin, and his team; my nephrologist, Dr. Fasika Tedla, and his team; the attending surgeons and physicians, nurses, techs, administrators, and personal care assistants; the Transplant Intensive Care Unit; the Surgical Intensive Care Unit; the ninth floor liver-kidney unit; my physical, occupational, speech and swallow therapists; the acute care wing and the nurses, techs, and personal care assistants; those that worked in nutrition, social work, pharmacy, and to all those that touched my life in departments and roles of which I know nothing: you are the community of the world that saved my life in enduring acts of love. I can only say that my love for you endures.

Introduction
Anticipation and Reality

Expecting is the greatest impediment to living. In anticipation of tomorrow, it loses today.

—Lucius Seneca, Stoic Philosopher—

Anticipation must inevitably come into confrontation with reality. Anticipation manifests itself in different ways in each day or season of life. People go to work with an anticipation that is lined with optimism, pessimism, or apathy. Perhaps a big account will close. Maybe that promotion will come. Maybe a dismissal or reprimand awaits. On that very same day, others anticipate that a loved one will slip from their embrace either to move on with life or to be carried away by death. That first cup of coffee in the morning, an expected visit from a friend, or the next dip in the roller coaster that one is on; these, too, are filled with the meaning of the word anticipation. Life is filled with so many moments of anticipation. Large, tiny, and those average and in-between.

Anticipation must always confront reality. It is triumphant at times; that is, it meets or exceeds anticipated expectations. At others, often more the case than not, it doesn't match the hype in one's thoughts and bones. In extreme cases, a concretely held sense of anticipation can be defeated by unforeseen outcomes. There may be, in real terms, evidence present that fortifies anticipation of positive outcomes, and yet disaster moves in, encamps, entrenches, and refuses to leave the scene.

Early on the morning of October 29, 2019, my wife, Nancy, and I, along with my living liver donor, Jackie, and her husband, Pete, together

Introduction

with our children left the Transplant Living Center of Mount Sinai Hospital and began our twenty-minute walk toward the hospital, through dark, deserted Manhattan streets. Anticipation was high that day for Jackie, me, and our spouses. You see, things were going to be better. I was going to receive a necessary, life-giving, and life-prolonging liver transplant that I desperately needed, and Jackie was going to see how one life given in kindness and selflessness could transform another. Adrenaline was flowing. I think that a chemical high from adrenaline more than anything else carried my jaundiced, swollen, pain-ridden, and terminally ill body to the admission ward at Mount Sinai. In my mind, nothing bad or tragic was going to happen. My life was going to be much better when all this was over. I was eager to get on with it. Had I known what the reality was going to be, my pace would have been much slower and more considered. I might even have turned back around and walked quickly in the opposite direction from Mount Sinai Hospital. There was no such prophetic insight, and vedic gifts became veiled by the rush of promise and tomorrow of hope.

The hospital came into sight and stood there, like a mountain in the sea of other mountains, stone and steel of human ingenuity containing the best of the best in medical arts. I would enter this mountain at its base. Little did I know that this was going to be the climb of my life, and it would be an impossible ascent followed by a hellish descent before my feet would touch again the pavement on which I stood that late October morning. For the next eight and one-half months, this was going to be my home.

My family and I lived for a few years in Croatia, where I taught at the Protestant seminary while working with the Reformed Church in Croatia and completing a doctorate in theology at Charles University in Prague. The term that Croatians use for hospital is *bolnica,* literally translated as *place of pain.* This is what Mount Sinai was to be for me in the coming months, a place of pain. It wasn't only that, of course, but that was to be the preponderance of my experience.

It may be of help to let you know how I came to be in the position of being terminally ill. When I was a young man around twenty years old, I was diagnosed with ulcerative colitis, an auto-immune disease effecting the intestinal track. It is painful, but it can be kept in control with medication. Certainly, the medications now are far more advanced than when I was diagnosed. Still, with the medications I was given as a young man, the disease, while painful and inconvenient, allowed me to get on with life.

Introduction

At thirty-two, I was diagnosed with another incurable and less treatable disease: primary sclerosing cholangitis or PSC. This is a liver disease associated with ulcerative colitis that causes inflammation and scarring of the bile ducts, the vessels that drain bile out of the liver. As the disease progresses, the ducts become compromised. It is essentially a plumbing problem as the backed-up bile cannot drain, and the liver is slowly destroyed. Nancy and I were told at that appointment that there was no treatment, just to wait until I needed a liver transplant. Needless to say, we were both stunned. They put me on a medication they hoped would thin the bile in the meantime, and for the next twenty-plus years, we were anticipating this next thing, this next big, life-threatening thing, to come along. That day came into focus in 2014 when my gastroenterologist called to inform us that my condition had progressed to full-on cirrhosis of the liver.

Because of the many ethical issues involved, the allocation of transplant organs is governed by the United Network for Organ Sharing system, or UNOS. For liver transplants, the scoring mechanism developed to help ensure that available organs go to the patients with the greatest need is known as the Model for End-Stage Liver Disease, or MELD, score. To be listed in the system for a transplant, the MELD score must be 15 or higher. For comparison, a normal person's score would be about 4, and about 40 is the highest it can go before death. Once I reached the stage of full cirrhosis, my score was 12. It would be years and more additional damage to my liver before I reached the necessary score to get into the transplant system.

Once a person is listed with UNOS, however, they are at the bottom. Time on the list, severity of illness, and blood type dictate movement upward. I have the very common Type-O blood, putting me in the longest line. Also, UNOS is divided by region. In New York, to get a liver from a deceased donor, your MELD score generally has to be higher than 30. Many people die before they reach the top of the list. This explains why the late Steve Jobs, the founder of Apple, bought a house in Tennessee, a region in which organs are more available.

The amazing thing, however, is that someone can donate a part of her liver to a person in need, and then the partial liver in the recipient and the remaining liver in the donor regenerate to a normal size and function. Truly a marvel! Furthermore, if a living donor designates someone to be the recipient, then that is who the recipient shall be. This is what we anticipated, but this would not be the end reality.

Introduction

What you will find in this book is not a chronological play-by-play of what happened although those elements are present. For the most part, this is my reflection about what happened to me, what I went through. It is about people who interacted with me during the eight and a half months I was at Mount Sinai Hospital in Manhattan and the months following my discharge. It is about the struggle I went through and still go through today.

I reflect as a patient for that is what I was. I reflect as a theologian for that is who I am and what I do. I reflect as a husband and father because I have a wife and children who were impacted as they watched their husband and father slip away. I reflect as a pastor because I was supported without hesitation and with passion by congregations I served then, had served in the past, and remarkably that I would serve! I reflect as a broken human for that is what I was and still am to this day. I reflect as a Christian because I believe in a God who has made humanity the divine *prima causa*. We have to do with a God who suffers, and this I believe is the great lodestone of contemplation Christianity brings as a gift for those who suffer in this life. And that of course is all of us.

If you seek here an answer to the eternal question of *why is there suffering?*, that is, *if God is both all-good and all-powerful then why is there suffering at all?*, if this is your question, I am afraid you will be disappointed. Theologians with minds far keener than mine have searched in vain for that chimerical answer. The only insight I have is that we have to do with a God that suffers with us and in doing so has brought the wreckage of humanity into God's selfhood. Should God become fully apprehended by us, yet another paradox would emerge: *can a God apprehended fully by humanity be God at all?* One thing that was solidified for me in my time at Sinai was the concept that God is wholly other and that I am human and therefore a toddler in the cosmos.

Some of what is contained here was written within a few weeks of my release. In these chapters, you may sense a rawness, vulnerability, and frailty. At times those chapters may seem incongruous with the rest of the offerings, and yet their very raw state may be revealing, and so I thought it important to work these in as I could. In my first eight months out, I was exceptionally frail, in body, mind, and spirit. Throughout the term in the hospital, my life was in the balance in all respects.

Mount Sinai is filled with allusion to that place in the Hebrew canon where Moses came face-to-face with God, where God's name was revealed, and where God revealed divine laws to humanity to govern our conduct.

Introduction

They are rules which have survived the test of time. I don't have any profound glimpse of heaven for you. I give you here no trumpet blowing, no angelic presence, no Jesus beckoning me home, no white light to follow. Still, I think I did touch the veil of death. I did touch upon divine majesty and mystery. I will address some of this. But when one has touched divine mystery, language is both unsuited and inadequate to convey otherness, holiness, and harmonic unity. It is simply beyond linguistic expression. The best I can hope to accomplish in this respect is to reflect from what is best understood as a borderland of death. I would express it theologically as a "no-man's land" between the terrestrial and celestial, something, perhaps *in-betweenness*, as understood in the concept of Sheol found in the Hebrew canon. What became apparent to me was the role of suffering, at least the place it has had in my journey and perhaps the journey of others.

While I can't say I came across angels, some beings were present that I cannot explain. These were beyond mere hallucinations although I had those, too. I merely think it is hubris and presumption to label them "angels" in the ordinary usage of the term or construct of the concept. What I can say is that my odyssey at Mount Sinai involved a precipitous climb, and for me, there is a powerful aspect of the holy about it all. What I had anticipated didn't come to pass, and what came to pass couldn't have been anticipated by anyone. Anticipation must always confront reality.

Prologue

Each friend represents a world in us, a world not born until they arrive, and it is only by this meeting that a new world is born.

—Anaïs Nin—

Jeri and I get up each morning sometimes with no incident but sometimes after a night filled with pain and night terrors. Almost without deviation, after I put my hearing aids in, we share a time of Pop-Tarts, coffee, and news, usually *Morning Joe*, unless something of utmost necessity intervenes. We head off to the bathroom after that, up the stairs, step after step, with which I struggle since I cannot sense my feet very well. I brush my teeth while Jeri sits on the counter next to the sink. Sometimes we talk, sharing about the struggle we survived, albeit wounded and changed. He looks at me with kind, understanding eyes.

We make the bed. It used to take a long time, maybe fifteen minutes. But we did it. It's easier now but still not an easy task. Jeri stays in bed most of the day. He waits. He's good at waiting in bed. Jeri is a bed warrior. He knows well the suffering, the languishing, the terror, and the loneliness that a bed can bring. Jeri and I know something else.

Things planned with precision often end in chaos. Jeri and I both bear signs and scars on our bodies of the onslaught. From time to time, we cry as we remember. Truthfully, there are many things that only Jeri and I know. No one else ever will, nor could they, even if I, with all the powers of expression, tried to explain. It simply would not translate.

Jeri is a stuffed bear given to me by my living donor, Jackie. His name came from a discussion between my wife, Nancy, and church administrator, Shari, after the initial transplant. Nancy struggled with how to refer to that portion of the liver that was Jackie's and was now in me. Shari came up with the *J* for *Jackie* and the *eri* for *Eric*. It was now both: *Jeri*. And so, it was only natural for Jeri to take on himself the name of a shared liver, he who was given as a get-well token and has grown to be so much more.

Through the night and in the morning, Nancy is with us. Jeri sleeps between Nancy and me. Nancy often wakes us in the middle of night terrors. When we first came home, Jeri and I needed the door to our bedroom open, and Nancy made sure this happened. The night terrors in many instances took us back to where we came from, to where we were remade, to the place of our tortuous and labyrinthine rescue, to the place where my life was snapped in two.

Jeri and I cannot escape that time or place either in body, mind, or spirit. I suppose we would like to. Maybe this is part of the reason we like the door open. Maybe someday we can walk through it. Maybe we can be free of it all. I think we all have events like that, times when we would just like to walk through the door and be rid of it all, Houdini-like to escape it. Nancy tends to things like that, makes sure we keep going, marshaling on, living for others and ourselves, living to re-member ourselves, living to speak again of the grace of God that both hides and makes declaration in the midst of suffering. This is life in the terrestrial arena: cryptic, esoteric, hermetic, daunting.

I spent my former life learning, plunging deep into the acroamatic nature of life, sacred scripture, and aspects of the divine. More recently my life was spent living in between life and death. I inhabited a borderland. There I grappled day and night in a contest of will and withdrawal, faith and suspicion. In those eternal moments, theory met praxis in this borderland between life and death. I lived there hour by hour, minute by minute.

Minutes can be unforgiving. I lived hundreds of thousands of such minutes. Minutes that drew out into an eternity and minutes that refused to budge or to pass on in the regular course of time. Eternity is contained in each minute, and each minute contains eternity. These minutes were filled with pain, with despair, with tears, and with groaning. These minutes left me hanging, for the longest time, between life and death, dying yet unable to die.

Many times, Jeri and I thought about how to escape our circumstances, planned for it in detail, and hallucinated about it. We never did escape. Instead, on July 10, 2020, Jeri and I progressed into the light of an overcast day on Madison Avenue in New York City. We had spent exactly eight and one-half months at Mount Sinai Hospital.

I

Jackie—My Living Donor

No one has greater love than this, to lay down one's life for one's friends.
—Jesus—

Getting a liver transplant in New York state without a living donor means you will be critical and near death before it happens, if it happens at all. New York has a shortage of organs for transplant and a long list of those needing them. For the truly fortunate, a living person will volunteer to undergo potentially life-threatening surgery to slice off a significant portion of a major organ in the hope of keeping you alive.

Because of the many ethical issues involved, the allocation of transplant organs in the United States is governed by the United Network for Organ Sharing, or UNOS, which uses the Model for End-Stage Liver Disease score to help ensure that organs go to the patients with the greatest need. For comparison, the MELD score ranges from about 4, for a non-diseased person, up to about 40, the highest it could go before death. In New York state, livers from deceased donors generally go to people with scores above 30. To be listed for transplant in the UNOS system, the score must be 15 or higher, and then the person enters at the bottom. Time on the list, severity of illness, and blood type dictate movement upward. Those with Type-O blood, like mine, are in the longest line.

When I first informed my congregation in Red Hook, New York, in 2014 that I had cirrhosis of the liver, my MELD score was 12, relatively low, and we were simply waiting for the number to climb high enough for me to be placed on the transplant list, an inevitable situation we had known for years was coming. We didn't know it then, but it would be another three years, in December 2017, before my number finally met the criteria, and I was listed for transplant. This was the demarcation that allowed testing for a potential living donor to begin.

Less than two days after I told my congregation at St. John's Reformed Church that I had been listed, a parishioner came to my office with an offer that stunned me. Her name is Jackie Fenaroli. Jackie had served as the assistant administrator during an earlier part of my tenure at St. John's. Jackie is always bubbly, smiling, effervescent. She is always ready to help those in need. I observed this on many occasions during my time at St. John's.

When Jackie came to my office, she burst out, "I want to do it. I want to be your donor!" I was taken aback. I am rarely at a loss for words, but I must confess this declaration left me speechless for a moment. I said that Nancy was planning on being tested first, to see if she could be my donor. Jackie understood that but then said if Nancy didn't work out, she wanted to do it. I thought about this act a great deal, and I thought about what Jesus had said, and what Jesus underwent in the end. This was not the act of someone running an errand for someone, visiting someone, or helping someone with food or clothing. This was an act concerning life and death. Donors can, and have, died attempting this. Every precaution is taken to protect the donor, of course, but it is not an uncomplicated matter to remove a huge chunk of a vital organ. I was simply stunned.

Nancy wanted dearly to be my donor. She saw it as a divine call. But this did not work out. She was disqualified. That was a hard setback for us. Again, Jackie extended the offer, only more vigorously this time. She began the process but was sadly disqualified as well.

Then my son and daughters thought about this too. They all wished to help. But I didn't want this for any of my children. I didn't want it for anyone. I thought about losing them, and how that alone would all but kill me. I thought about doomsday scenarios. What if they survived but developed difficulties afterward. Could I live with that? My son, Samuel, was the first to approach me. I told him no; I didn't want him to be a donor. He insisted.

The thing to know about Samuel is how ruthlessly logical he is. He is not rude, coarse, or uncaring. He is a happy, gentle soul. We named him after the biblical Samuel, whose name means "God has heard." I find it hard sometimes to understand the extent of the blessing God granted to me in this child. The same can be said of Valerie and Penelope.

The argument that finally tripped me up was when he said, "Dad, if you died, and I hadn't done everything I could do to save you, how do you think I would feel for the rest of my life?" I really couldn't hold back my tears because my dad was dying at the time. Samuel also asked if I wouldn't do this for my dad, and further, if I wouldn't insist on doing so for him. These were all salient points. So he began the process. When my care was transferred from Westchester Medical Center to Mount Sinai, it was found that Samuel had the same blood condition as Nancy and was therefore disqualified as a donor.

Mount Sinai took another look at Jackie, and amazingly she was determined to be a suitable and sound donor. In the early autumn of 2019, Jackie came by the parsonage with the news that Mount Sinai had approved her as my donor. After all the years of waiting, the light had finally turned green! I remember how excited she was. We all were. It did not take long for Mount Sinai to schedule the surgery. October 29, 2019, was set as the day. Jackie, the persistent, effervescent one, knew she was going to be my donor. I think she knew this even when Westchester had rejected her.

I wondered about what her husband, Pete, and her children, Matt and Gianna, were thinking about this. Pete told me that when Jackie got the idea to do something, he pitied the person who got in her way. They all supported her in what she was doing. They knew who Jackie was; they knew the lengths she would go to help someone. I have often said of Jackie that she is the type of person who would push you out of the way of an oncoming bus, knowing full well that she would not clear its path.

As a pastor, I long to have this sort of love, and I work for it and toward it. Jackie has it in her system, like some form of divine virus. The Apostle Paul describes love like this, "Love is patient; love is kind . . . It does not insist on its own way . . . It bears all things, believes all things, hopes all things, endures all things" (1 Cor 13:4–7). That passage is read at weddings a lot. But Paul is referring to a love that transcends. Indeed, it can and should abide in a marriage, but Paul is talking about a special love, *agape*, in the Greek of the New Testament. It is this divine, transcendent love that supersedes all other gifts. *Agape* is the gift Jackie has. The way it was expressed toward me was that Jackie underwent *voluntary, major surgery* to have more than half of a vital organ removed to give it to me so that I could have the *chance* to continue living. She had to endure pain to do that, pain without knowing what the outcome would be. She had a long period of recovery, and she even had to have some additional procedures to correct some things. That's *agape*.

Jackie, both before the transplant and after, did something further. She read a great deal about the whole process. She, at any given moment, probably knew more of what was going on than I did. She sought information for us. She remembers significant milestones in all the events that took place and sends me reminders of them.

In the end, I did not come home with Jackie's liver. But I am convinced that Jackie saved my life. Because I had a living donor, I was under the medical care I needed at the time I needed it. Things didn't turn out as we thought, but I'm alive because someone with much planning and forethought put her life on the line for me.

Doctors put 60 percent of Jackie's liver in me, but my body simply needed more as it quickly developed what they call small-for-size syndrome. I think I was just much sicker than they anticipated, and the partial liver simply could not keep up with all the backed-up bile and built-up toxins in my system. That bile, seeking anywhere to go, had taken over any available vessel and enlarged my spleen to many times its normal size. That pressurized spleen was pouring blood into this new tiny liver at such a rate that they had to do a procedure a couple of days later to slow it down. My kidneys also became overwhelmed and failed shortly after the transplant, another major setback attributed to the stress of surgery and/or high levels of anti-rejection medication. As days passed, multiple complications piled up, one on another. By mid-December, my MELD score had climbed to 35, and I was listed for a second transplant, this time for both a full liver and a kidney, which would necessarily have to come from the same deceased donor. (I was told because of my blood type, I would be fourth or fifth in line.) Despite all that, Jeri, the transplanted liver from Jackie, had grown to normal size in a matter of about ten weeks. Signs of necrosis had begun, but Jeri kept me alive until that second transplant could happen—exactly ninety days after the first one.

I'm not sure how Jackie herself felt when it was apparent that the transplant had failed. I'm not sure what she must have felt when the person she laid her life down for was dying. I can only imagine that this was a heavy burden. She and Pete visited me every time she came to Manhattan for an appointment, and in fact, they were present just before they took me down for the second transplant as she was there for her three-month checkup. She had to bear all things related to her donation, even the prospect that it had all been for naught. She had to endure that. I imagine that her effervescence may have been injured in all of this. Her laying down of her life went far beyond just laying down her life; she also had to pick up the burdens associated with that decision.

Even though I don't carry Jackie's liver, I hope I carry a small part of something far rarer than that. I hope part of the *agape* that Jackie has was transplanted into my heart.

2

Death Begets Life—My Deceased Donor

I still don't know why she died, and I lived. I don't know the answer to nothin', not a blessed thing.

—MAC SLEDGE IN *TENDER MERCIES*—

In the days of late December and through January, things were bleak. I needed a full liver and a kidney transplant if I was going to survive. Encephalopathy was sending neurotoxins to my brain because my diseased liver could not filter them out. Delusions and hallucinations haunted me. An infection developed and sent me into a coma on December 30. I was living in the borderland between life and death. At no point did I feel like I was unconscious, my mind active and interacting with what was happening to my body. I even remember talking about this second transplant and trying to communicate that I just couldn't endure it (though my wife says those communications actually happened weeks after the second transplant). I hallucinated that my family and I had gathered on a Sunday, a chance to laugh and love. Then I had to say goodbye because they wanted to send me away for another surgery, and I didn't want to leave. I wanted those moments to last. I remember that loved ones came and, in fact, gathered around me on the day of that second transplant. Present were Nancy, always Nancy; Samuel, my son and his spouse, Jack; and Jackie, my living donor, and her husband, Pete. Jackie was at Mount Sinai for her three-month check-up as my second transplant happened exactly ninety days after the first one.

Death had been in pursuit and presented many obstacles to be overcome. Before the second transplant happened, Nancy was twice offered organs on my behalf. Once I was disqualified due to infection. I actually sprouted a stream of fluid like a fountain from my previous surgical wound. All told, they would collect some eight liters of sepsis-filled fluid that day. The second time, an issue with the organs themselves made them unviable. Discouragement came each time for my family. It was becoming clear to all who could see me that I couldn't wait much longer. But then it came, and none too soon. On January 27, it happened. I was taken into surgery for a transplant of liver and kidney.

In my soul to this day, it is the cause of a great and grievous struggle. One of the complicating factors in this is my son, Samuel. As of this writing, Samuel is 28 years old. He holds a master's in library and information sciences and works as a librarian at Princeton University. He is married to his wonderful partner, Jack, who is a student at Princeton Theological Seminary. I say this certainly as a proud parent, but I say it also as a patient who on that miraculous day received a life-saving kidney and liver from someone who died.

The donor system is such that the anonymity of the donor and their family is preserved. So, I know very little about my donor. What I do know is that my donor was a male, aged 27, who died on Long Island. That was just a couple of years older than my Samuel at that time.

Samuel had also gone through the process of seeing if he could donate. I wasn't in favor of this. I told him that it was risky and that if I lived and through some unforeseen complication, I awoke to find that he had died, I would die also at that moment. Perhaps not bodily although that would also be a possibility given what I now know about the power of the soul. My soul would have withered; my heart would have wilted. My life from that tragedy would have been one of self-torture, a torment, a twisted testimony that I could not live with. Samuel persisted and I, with reluctance, relented. However, Samuel didn't make the cut. In so many ways, that was a relief to me.

When I think of my donor, I think of Samuel. Male, the same age, at the beginning of life. Hope, promise, the future before him. My heart fades, and my eyes fill with tears when I think of my deceased donor, the end of his life, and the tragedy his family had to endure. I think of this every day and often. I cannot begin to unravel the mystery of this: why he died, and I lived. People who have good intentions say to me that God must have a purpose for me. Perhaps, but what of the purpose for my donor? There is a randomness and incongruity in the providence of God that is a bewildering parable for me. Why did he die, and I live? I had had a full life, even at my then-57 years of age. I wonder how he died. I wonder about his family and their grief in the wake of the loss of their young son. I weep, and there is a rain inside my soul that will never stop. Part of him is me now. Was he married? Did he have children? They would be so young. Who was he? What was he? What did he want from life?

Such a sacrifice is immeasurable. I wonder, if the situation were reversed, if I could give away part of Samuel if he met a tragic end. This family did. They made that decision along with their dead son. January 27 comes for me, marking the day that I began a long journey from death to life. It marks a day of rejoicing for my family. But somewhere on Long Island, January 26 marks a day of profound sadness, a day of immense loss, a loss that marks not only that day but every day of their lives. The question for them must be inscrutable. I wonder, what if he had lived? What would he have become, what would he have experienced? Such a sacrifice is an act of love toward a stranger. The family would have no idea if I were a good person or a scoundrel. It is a risk to love like that, love without knowing, love without judgment. Loving a stranger is both formidable and arduous.

The author of Hebrews says: "Do not neglect to show hospitality to strangers, for by doing that some have entertained angels without knowing it" (Heb 13:2). I am no angel; that is a certitude. But the first part of this verse brings things home. Just before this verse, we see the governing idea behind it: "Let mutual love continue" (Heb 13:1). Love takes wing in the form of hospitality to strangers. Luke Timothy Johnson, in his commentary on Hebrews, says that hospitality is "a concrete expression of mutual love."[1] Johnson further observes, "The point for the hearers of this discourse is clear: they must be willing to extend hospitality to all strangers for they can never know what manner of visitation from God the strangers might bring."[2] The word for hospitality is an interesting one. *Philoxenias* (φιλοξενίας). It rightly translates to hospitality, but if we break it apart it means love of strangers (*philo*-love and *xenia*-strangers). The love of strangers. I find it

---

1. Luke Timothy Johnson, *Hebrews A Commentary* (Louisville: Westminster John Knox, 2006), 339.

2. Johnson, *Hebrews*, 340.

truly baffling the number of commentaries that catch the love aspect of this passage but limit the scope of the love or fail to mention the *stranger* part of the word. I think this is critical. It certainly became critical for me that someone had high regard for a stranger and exercised an extreme act of *brotherly love (philadelphia)*, a word also used in these two verses, and a word rather peculiar to the early Christian community.

The church father John Chrysostom in his commentary demonstrates the relation of hospitality to love. He remarks that the author of Hebrews "did not say, 'Do not neglect to entertain strangers,' but 'to show hospitality'; that is, do not merely entertain strangers, but do it with love for the strangers." This, I think, is the correct understanding of what the author is trying to convey.

In our culture when we speak of hospitality, we usually think of it as entertaining. Inviting someone to dinner, or letting a friend spend the night while on a journey. In the Christian community, we might also see this as providing meals in a soup kitchen for the poor or supporting a homeless shelter. These are certainly all forms of hospitality, but the author of Hebrews, I think, is digging for something deeper, something more sacrificial on the part of the Christian community. I have no idea what the early Christian community might have thought about organ transplantation. My guess is that they may have thought that it was an ugly and unnatural practice because of their firm belief in the resurrection of the body and the sacredness of the body of each individual.

Today, however, with the exception of a few sects of Christianity, blood and organ donations are part and parcel of how we live. I view the body to be a sacred thing, too. Its dignity should be defended and preserved. But because the body is sacred, the surrender of it to preserve the life of another—as in the case of both my living and deceased donors—is itself a sacred act of sacrifice. I am a firm believer in the resurrection of the body. I also have the realization that God has a lot of sorting to do to make that happen. I don't know what that resurrected body will be. I am Lazarus, not Christ.

The body I have now is not all mine, at least in the sense that major organs that provide life are not the ones I was born with. A part of someone else resides in me. That's not just a strange thought; it's a strange feeling. I can still feel where I was cut in my abdomen. There is a loss of nerve function there that feels odd, so I am always aware of it. There are parts of me that are emotionally different, too. Some of this has to do with the ordeal, of course. But I also have a sense that a part of me is gone and something new and different stands there in its place. My tastes are different. Different things bother me. There is a less resilient side of me. I would even say that there is a vulnerability, a sensitivity that is there now, that wasn't there before. I think that I feel things more deeply. I hold these to be sacred gifts the stranger within gave to me.

I have come to realize, too, there is a curious form of hospitality going on inside of me. My body had to welcome a stranger. Our bodies have immediate, negative, and powerful reactions to foreign entities. The first reaction is to fight and to do so with the intention to kill. The physicians had to pump many immunosuppressants into my system because it is an inhospitable environment for "the stranger." It has to be formed into a hospitable environment in order for the "other" to survive. For the rest of my life, I will have to take medications morning and night to maintain a hospitable environment for the strange organs.

The author of Hebrews, perhaps, knew that the natural tendency of a community is to shun, exile, harm, or even kill the stranger and that the church might find the stranger threatening. Hospitality, in the way Scripture understands it, is difficult. It grinds against natural inclinations, and it demands daily attention to the command to never forget to love the stranger because one never knows when a visitation of God may come on account of it. The church in so many ways needs a healthy dose of immunosuppressants; that is, it needs a daily dose of *philoxenia*. We are not adept or practiced at the art of scriptural *philoxenia*. We attack and offer only an inhospitable environment when the stranger may be bearing the gift of divine visitation.

I've thought of my transplant in this way. A stranger came, and God visited me with the gift of an extended life, extended time with my family and friends, and extended time in God's creation. But I view it all differently now, more transient and fleeting than ever. The Apostle Paul has rightly said that we are aliens (strangers!) and sojourners in this world. Nevertheless, we are tied to it and exist in it, and I am thankful for the time that has been granted to me. I also think of my donor and his family who extended these things to me, a stranger. They imparted to me hospitality, a love for a stranger, at great loss to themselves. How ponderous this was and is to them. I ache for their loss and know that I cannot comprehend it.

I can only live and pray for my donor and his family. I want to live well, and to that, I am obliged. I pray and ask and hope that somehow because they have ministered to me with extravagant hospitality, that even in loss, they will experience the visitation of God.

3

Food Fights

Let food be your medicine, and medicine your food.
—Hippocrates—

Food, glorious food. We take it for granted, most of us. We eat on the run, on the street, and from bags passed through car windows. Whatever it is, it keeps us going. Food became an enemy for me in November 2019. My new liver was overwhelmed. They tried corrective measures and surgeries as well as dialysis to try and "jump start" my kidneys, but nothing worked.

Nourishment was vitally important. After all, I was supposed to be growing a liver. There was a point when it became difficult for me to eat, and in the end impossible. I knew I needed to eat, but something wasn't right inside me. Food and I simply wanted nothing to do with each other. My aversion to food became an arena of combat between me and those around me.

At some point, it seemed that each person who walked through my hospital room's door had an agenda, and that agenda was to get me to eat something, anything. The problem was that food nauseated me and each time I ate, I would gag or vomit, or both. This would happen immediately or fifteen to twenty minutes after I ate. Even the mention of food was nausea-invoking. I have never had difficulty eating, so this was something new to me. Nancy was constantly pushing me to eat. Then my daughters. Everyone was saying, "Eat! You need to eat." It wore on me. There was Nancy, echoing Mrs. Claus in the Rankin/Bass production of "Rudolf the Red-Nosed Reindeer," constantly pushing on a rather thin Mr. Claus to "Eat, Santa, eat!"

It was as if everyone thought I was willfully refusing to eat. But the problem went much deeper than that. I thought that a psychological and physiological breakdown was taking place inside me. I thought that this had something to do with my mind. I began to think that if I could just repair the psychological breakdown, I would be able to eat. I dove deep into myself to try and fix it. I simply couldn't.

In my machinations, it also occurred to me that perhaps this would never be right. I might not ever be able to eat or even like food again. Still, the pressure came. Eat, eat, you need to eat. Nausea upon nausea at each call to eat. Vomit followed every attempt to do so. Eventually, I became angry. Angry because I couldn't fix it; angry because people wouldn't let me be. I longed for orders for me to be put on NPO (meaning nothing by mouth) for testing, simply because it meant that for several hours people would cease their pleading with me to eat. Then the doctors told me they might have to insert a tube to feed me. It would run from my nose to my stomach, providing nourishment. I didn't want that.

I had had a tube running from my nose to my stomach before. I remember it was awful. It became so disagreeable to me that I pulled it out. The memories of this were not fond ones. When the doctors told me that unless I ate, they would need to insert one of these tubes in me, naturally I revolted at the idea. I redoubled my effort but to no avail. During this period, as in all periods, I was in intense pain, and I was delusional. It was all surreal.

Eventually, I consented to letting the feeding tube be inserted. I did know that I had to have nutrition. So began a steady diet of Nepro, a nutritional shake designed especially for people on dialysis. When the tube was originally inserted, it was on a "trickle feed" and considered only as supplemental nutrition, so I was still encouraged to eat by everyone. Constant as spring rain. I would implore visitors not to argue with me about food. I didn't want the whole visit to be a nutritional disputation. I knew quite well I needed to eat. I knew quite well that I wasn't able to. Eating equaled nausea.

My internal logic was that the substance from the tube would stay down unless I tried to eat, in which case I would lose both the food I was trying to eat and the Nepro from the tube. Simply reduced, if I didn't try to eat, I retained the Nepro; if I tried to eat, I lost both. My conclusion was that it was better to have something rather than nothing. Stop talking about it. Stop arguing with me. I know I need to eat. Can we just visit? It took so much energy for me to argue. I knew what they were trying to do. I knew their motives were good, but I grew so utterly weary of it all.

I hallucinated too. I thought that what was inside me was a contraption made of wood that looked like a water mill, spilling Nepro into my stomach. Not in my right mind, I began to start to pull on the tube. I thought it was interfering with my breathing. I thought that not only I, but others, had this machine in them and that we needed to pull it out. I hallucinated that other patients were asking me to do this, that this would be our protest against our inability to breathe properly. I know that on several occasions I succeeded in removing the tube, which led to the discomfort of having medical staff reinsert it. Then before they could restart the feeding, there would be a delay of several hours because they had to bring up the imaging device to make sure it was placed correctly. Each time I pulled it out, I lost a day's worth of calories. Eventually calls for me to eat fell away as larger issues came to the fore. My diet for the rest of my journey was whatever came through that tube in my nose. I never could have guessed I would live on that form of nutrition for more than six additional months. Up until the last weeks of my hospitalization, I would be fed only by tube. I lost weight. I'm not a big man to begin with; my normal weight being less than 150 pounds. By the time of my release, I was down to eighty-five pounds.

When the calls to eat fell away, so did my nausea. I worked on what I thought was a psychological problem. I wept day after day for what I thought might be a permanent condition of loathing food, even the thought of it. I also knew at that point that something was desperately wrong. Things hadn't gone as expected. I was in trouble, and I knew it. My inability to consume food was part of it. But I also had an aversion to food. I was worried about this aversion being permanent. If I managed to live, would it be with a tube somewhere forever providing me with nourishment to survive with no joy or pleasure involved? It was a harrowingly inconceivable thought that I had never had to think about before.

In Exodus, the account of the Israelites having to eat manna every day as a means just to survive now strikes me differently. If year after year, survival was dependent upon eating the exact same food without variance, much is lost. The joyful part of eating is lost, and the desire for variation is not in reach. The pleasure to which we look forward to in eating eluded them. I understand this to an extent. We may read the account of their complaining and conjure a *tsk, tsk*, but this is to miss something. Scripture abounds in language concerning feast and festival. Food is celebrated and is a part of celebration. Good food, good wine, good life. Until it is not there. And when it is not there, life languishes, withers, and eventually dies. Variety also plays a part in the joy of food. No one wants to eat the same thing every day. This was where the complaint of the children of Israel comes into play. I wonder how long we would go without complaint having the same food every day for days, weeks, months, and years on end.

There is something about food that is mundane; that is, it is ordinary and circadian. However, every culture celebrates food and uses food in celebration. In the mundane resides the Holy. In my tradition, I think of the importance of our sacrament of Eucharist or Holy Communion. A common union of the human with the divine in the mundane elements of wine and bread, the central elements of my religious tradition. But if anyone had mentioned to me the notion of taking part in communion in the hospital, I would have been nauseated. It pains the soul. Usually, this sacrament carries with it connotations of healing and hope. I couldn't psychologically or physically have tolerated it. The sacred was also refused me in the absence of these elements.

In my denomination, we typically celebrate communion monthly. I see people as they partake in communion. It's a privilege of my office. I see tears of joy as well as indifference. I see those who are moving in a purely perfunctory manner and at times I can see those who carry with them an attitude of imposition at having been disturbed to come and partake at all. Others are hurt and angry at what life and perhaps God have brought to them. I understand that too.

Theologians and ministers are often so anxious to make sure that people understand we serve a loving, kind, and good God, that we rob God of another potentiality—darkness. For those of the Abrahamic faiths, we serve the God of plague and pestilence as well as the God of love. Often, we are keen to separate the love of God from the terror of the God of all that is. We are apt to want to put this out of the discussion, to forgive God from a human vantage point of these things. We wish to absolve God from all responsibility for the darkness, evil, and suffering that befall us. That is, we wish to praise God in times of food and festival but look to other scapegoats in times of hardship and crisis. This is to empty God of omnipotence. It is to say God only governs and provides the good, but somehow runs into a barrier and becomes impotent in the arena of darkness. I am a minister of the gospel of God's goodness, and I must confess, perhaps now more than ever before, this is the table I like to set.

In the Christian faith, we run into horrible and corrupt theologies that would bless people who seem blessed in worldly terms but curse those who are suffering or struggling mightily in this world. What an awful perfidy toward the gospel of Jesus Christ. In our highest, most sacred mystery of faith—communion—we are participating in a feast of *suffering*. The elements of Eucharist point to suffering: the breaking of Christ's body and the shedding of Christ's blood. It reminds us, too, that we are participating in Christ's complete passion: anguish, loneliness, sorrow, separation, the anticipation of pain, the excruciating pain, the torment of the soul. A feast. My tradition's communion liturgy, like many others, confesses: "This is a *feast* of hope, of remembrance, and of love." We are renewed in this feast because it indicates above all else that God is a God that has a *part* in our suffering but is also present *in* our suffering.

I was barred from this feast. Instead, my lament went something along the lines of that of the psalmist: "My mouth is dried up like a potsherd" (Ps 22:15). Holy Communion became an impossibility for me although I, perhaps more than many or most, needed the soulish nourishment of these mundane elements.

Eucharist, it's a word for communion most Protestants don't use. I suppose because it is "too Catholic." But the word *Eucharist* itself comes from the gospel accounts of Jesus celebrating Passover with his disciples before his Passion. "And when he had given thanks (ευχαριστησασ/*eucharistaisas*, Luke 22:19), he broke bread." *Eucharist*, it's a great word for what happens and what we should be doing, giving thanks. In my condition, I really wondered at times whether Eucharist would be possible anymore. More than this I wondered if I would ever be able to be a celebrant again, a Minister of Word and Sacrament. This, too, brought pain.

Months and months on a feeding tube. Then close to my release date, food was permitted, with an altered diet of course. I had to digest thick liquids because I was learning how to swallow again because of my tracheostomy—the hole cut in my throat to attach me to the ventilator—and subsequent damage to my esophagus. Food was spilling into my lungs instead of going to my stomach. Thick juice, thick milk. It wasn't very appetizing or appealing, but I was beginning my first steps, fighting my way back to eating. With my speech and swallow therapist, I began exercises for my throat, lungs, and speaking. I was working for the day that I would be able to swallow regular food, drink a cup of coffee, and eat a regular meal. I flunked the swallow test on several occasions, each one bringing a poignancy and a realization that my esophagus might never heal.

Days before my release I was taken to the lab to do a final swallow test. Apprehensiveness filled me. As the exam began, I knew I was not doing well. But, with all that was in me, I regrouped and remembered each exercise I had done. Then things began to come together. The therapist said I passed. I held my walker, leaned back against the wall, and cried. My therapist cried. A technician passed it down the unit, "he passed." I heard cheering and then clapping. I could swallow! I could enjoy food! I could drink coffee!

You might think that after this I might have a new appreciation of food. Not really. It's a daily thing I do, like everyone else. Mealtime blessings oftentimes seem perfunctory, something we do because we think we should. But now often I'm frozen in front of my meal. I hang my head. I remember, and I give thanks, truly and deeply.

I am functioning as a Minister of Word and Sacrament again. At times it's a real joy to be at the communion altar. At times I do feel myself falling backward when Eucharist in all the various applications of that word was impossible. I have to push through those times, the raw emotion *of then* springs into *the now*, and there I am with those mundane elements and a soul so full of suffering that I can hardly steer a clear course through the Words of Institution:

> Then he took a loaf of bread, and when he had given thanks, he broke it and gave it to them, saying, "This is my body, which is given for you. Do this in remembrance of me." And he did the same with the cup after supper, saying, "This cup that is poured out for you is the new covenant in my blood." (Luke 22:19-20)

Ever given, ever present.

It is not lost on me that the church has entered into food fights through the centuries. Most notably at the Reformation with Luther and Rome, and then Luther and Zwingli. Food fights over the Eucharist. It's awful when you think of it this way, but that's what we engaged in, food fights. It came down to who was going to be able to eat and who was not. To this day as a Protestant, I cannot partake of Eucharist with the Catholics nor participate in the Divine Mystery with the Orthodox. For the life of me, I cannot see the difference in the theological formulations of Alexander Schemmann (an Orthodox theologian) and John Calvin (the founder of Reformed Christianity). We don't throw food at each other; we throw words. And we fail to give thanks for each other. Food fights are often associated with the adolescent and the puerile. Quite a bit of anger was bandied about as well. I see that about the church now. We are adolescents of God throwing words about divine food. It's tragic and laughable.

My family and friends remember the days of our food fights. They remind me of how angry I was and the things I did and said. One incident in particular was so painful and poignant they found they had to laugh to keep from crying. I understand this too. It's kind of a release valve for them after a very serious encounter with crisis and tragedy. Still, it hurts. All that was going on in my body and mind, all that was hostage in my heart is ever-present.

At one point in my delirium, all I could think about was an ice-cold Coke. The kind that came in a glass bottle. I wanted it in a classic Coke glass, filled with ice, full of fizz that would tickle my nose. When more lucid, I would fill my Amazon cart with Coca-Cola products—glasses, napkins, coasters, etc., before deleting it. When I got home, there on the dresser in the room in which I was to recover, Nancy had placed a bottle of Coca-Cola next to a classic Coke glass. I wasn't so much longing for the Coke by that point, but I knew what it meant. I gave thanks that I was *able* to drink it. To this day I haven't. I hold on to it, the full bottle and the glass empty. I suppose it serves as a reminder that we sometimes have all that we ever need, while at others we pant like a deer that thirsts for running waters. Someday maybe I'll open it and pour it out into the glass. As sacrilegious as it sounds, I think that as I do so, I'll remember the words: "And when he had given thanks . . ." And they will echo in the deep recesses of my soul.

4

Delusions, Hallucinations, and Near-Death Experiences

A hallucination is a fact, not an error; what is erroneous is a judgment based upon it.

—BERTRAND RUSSELL—

From the first day of recovery until near my release date, I don't remember a day that wasn't filled with delusions or hallucinations. Even before being hospitalized, I had suffered from encephalopathy, a disease in the brain caused by a buildup of neurotoxins that my failing liver could not filter. It affected my concentration before the surgery but escalated afterward. Pain medications and the trauma of the surgeries also played a part in my struggle for mental equilibrium.

It's hard for me to make a distinction between delusions and hallucinations, but there is one. Delusions are closely tied to reality, and they are frequently attended by paranoia. At least they were for me. I suppose that's why when paranoid thought is present, it is referred to as delusional thinking. Hallucinations can reflect or provide a constructed parable for what is happening in reality, but it is more detached, a world unto itself.

This is not to say that hallucinations don't take place in real time and space. I had those too. I heard our dog barking. That's an auditory hallucination. I had many of these. I saw and spoke to people who were not in the room but were as real and concrete to me as others who truly were in the room with me. At times, people that existed in the real world were dragged into my hallucinogenic constructs, or world-building. My delusions and hallucinations were both quite real to me, and the things, people, and events that occurred in them exist in my memory as any other memory does. This constitutes part of my post-traumatic stress disorder, or PTSD.

The difficulty in writing about delusions and hallucinations is that words seem inadequate to capture in any meaningful way the power of the images and events they brought. In attempting to describe them, they take on a benign and mundane nature that does a great disservice to their concreteness and potency. The Apostle Paul talks about an otherworldly experience and says of it that he "heard things that are not to be told, that no mortal is permitted to repeat" (2 Cor 12:4). That's how I feel about my experiences of delusions, hallucinations, and near-death experiences. Except it's not that I'm not permitted to speak of them; it's that language fails to have ways to articulate what happened in those places with adequate color or depth. Still, I will try to convey at least a sense of what was happening to me.

To that end, delusions are perhaps the more easily recounted, as hallucinations defy depiction in many respects. Because they played an almost daily role in my hospitalization, I hope that I can in some way express the intensity of what went on. Part of the difficulty lies in the fact that I cannot give an accurate timeline of when these happened. I can now only guess what delusion or hallucination corresponds to which actual event, but there is, I am certain, a correlation.

The first hallucination that I remember is perhaps when I first regained some form of consciousness, after my first transplant. I saw nothing other than an immense black hole in front of me and thickness around me. The best analogy would be that it was like waking up in a coffin. My first thought was, "Am I dead?" The second was, "How would I know if I was dead?" It was terror anchored in my soul. There was nothing but a darkness and my consciousness, an awareness of myself. The debate raged in my head as the thick, impenetrable, darkness persisted. Then a third question came, "What is death?" I began going through theologians and philosophers that I was familiar with searching for an answer to "What is death?" This search seemed to go on interminably with no answer to be found. Then at length, I was debating with a French philosopher, real to me but an imagined personage. We were discussing his enormous yet totally imagined work, *Death and Time*. There was only a disembodied voice. I never saw the philosopher. I was exhausted from it all. I just wanted the thick darkness to end. Then the philosopher showed me an object floating amid the black that explained the intersection of time and death. That brought the war waging in my mind to rest.

I cannot answer to this day whether that was an experience of death or not. I don't think so, but how do I know? And if this is death or a part of it, then I understand why death is viewed as an enemy to be defeated. This understanding of death lies at the heart of Christian teaching. If this is death or a part of it, I have no desire to see it come anytime soon. Death is a dreaded enemy. Horrible, twisted, gargantuan, and I would not want to meet it without being accompanied by faith.

Faith is a fierce defender. A part of me leans toward an understanding that faith may be the very substance of life, something that pushes one through to life beyond this life. In the deepest recesses I think I argued with death because I believed profoundly that something had to exist beyond it. In the instance of this hallucination, it took a negative form: I disbelieved in death.

In an early delusion, I sensed that my stay was going to be unending. It turns out this was more than a little prescient. It wasn't just that I felt things were unceasing. There was a growing paranoia in me and a cycle of hallucinations both inwardly and outwardly that were adding to this particular delusion. In it, there was a growing religious community coming in and out of Mount Sinai that met in secret. I perceived them as genuinely good people, but cultish in nature, bizarrely so. They were distributing food rations to their community. Apparently, food was scarce, but through an arrangement with the government, this community managed to get food. They found that they could also help my congregation in Red Hook to receive the food they needed, too. It was all dystopian, as were most of my hallucinations and delusions. This was an ongoing scheme and one that eventually went wrong due to the dilapidated delivery machines and systems. They collapsed leaving people and the program in danger.

While this was happening, I believed the pulse oxygen monitor that was on my finger had been implanted with a coded chip, and I had been entrusted with the release of food to the underground community by transmitting the signal through this monitor. But the signal and its timing had to be perfect. I tapped my finger with its ET-like light, Morse-code style, to send a signal. I kept wondering, both in the real world to real people and in my hallucinations, why they would have put such an important task into the hands of someone so obviously ill-equipped to handle it. I tore at that thing to get it off, begged someone else to do this. I kept telling those around me that I didn't know how to do it. I asked if my donor's husband had relayed the message to Red Hook, seizing on him perhaps because I knew he was nearby and strong. Those around me were dumbfounded as I pulled at the monitor and repeatedly said I didn't know how to use it. They tried to reassure me that there was nothing I needed to do, and yet my obligation to my community seemed to rest on my finger's action.

Most of the time I just wanted out. These images just kept coming, relentlessly. I plotted with friends to get out. There was a helicopter and SUV involved, and I asked Nancy to have our son Samuel bring ropes and a grappling hook to latch onto my bed and yank me out. While I was in reality on the sixth floor in a room in which the windows did not open, in my delusional state, I was at street level and could, if the non-existent wooden blinds were twisted open, see the legs of people outside. Even my critical care nurse was to be involved in the escape.

Again, in the early stages, I thought that psychological experiments were being done on me. Interns would be set up behind two-way mirrors to observe and challenge patients. The Wi-Fi devices on the ceiling were crawling all over like huge beetles with their eyes and ears. They would put images on the TV screen (which was off in reality) to see what kind of response they could get. It was all very dark and nefarious. I would hear the sounds of people being beaten down the hallways. I heard a crash. I tried to get out of bed to help. I remember a nurse coming and telling me to lie still that everything was all right. The nurse recounted the story to Nancy the next day: a trash bin had fallen over, and the nurse thought that because I was a pastor, used to helping people, I was trying to go to the assistance of a person I thought had fallen.

The paranoia and hallucinations became worse. The staff was starting to splinter. Part of the staff was using techniques on transplant patients that were dangerous and highly questionable; part of the staff was using sound and proven medical techniques. There was a creature that the corrupt staff were using and experimenting on; it was gigantic and hirsute. They lifted it with a small crane. I found out it was a human suffering under their experimentation. The creature was loathsome, but beyond this, that creature was an image of God. While my skin crawled at the sight, my heart was told to love.

On their religious festal days, the villainous staff would distribute large lollipops filled with liquor to "treat" the patients assigned to them.

This was, of course, not the most salutary thing to do with liver transplant patients. Then there was an entire drug ring that they ran. They made the substance in a laboratory down the hall. I would see them going in and out. My daughters were pulled into this scheme. I tried to tell Nancy the girls were in trouble, in grave danger. I couldn't seem to convince her; she would only tell me everything was all right. But in my world, it wasn't. Sometimes this odious staff would be assigned to me. It was then that fear would rise in me. I had no control over who did, or did not, provide treatment to me in this hallucinogenic mix of people.

At some point, I was transported to a small storefront sort of clinic. It was a tourist area and people came to have fun and drink, especially the younger people. I wasn't in Florida at Daytona Beach. I think I felt like I was in the Appalachian region. The clinic was small but very full of patients. I was one of them yet recovering from a major procedure—a liver transplant! But in the transfer, all my information had been lost, and I didn't have any identification. They thought I was just a tourist who had done too many drugs, had too many drinks, and had come to solicit sex from the prostitutes there. Again, I was scared, full of anxiety at every moment.

Even as these things were going on, I was still somewhat cognizant of what was happening to me. For quite a while I was even able to respond correctly (or near correctly) about where I was. Although, given this hallucination, I no longer believed I was at Mount Sinai, I just told them what they wanted to hear. But in most of these hallucinations, I did think that at least the personnel were associated with the hospital, that Mount Sinai had set up little affiliate clinics everywhere.

One such clinic was next door to the clinic I was in. They had found my paperwork and transferred me. But this affiliate was struggling financially, so it was a clinic during the day but a boutique that held fashion shows at night. I was allowed to stay at night, but in a corner, squirreled away as it were. I could see the fashion show but the models were wearing a mask that resembled the ones fencers wear. Those masks would at times rub up against my face, some were smooth and pleasing, others rough and disagreeable. Again, anxiety and dread at each moment. Again, these images were tied into the earlier ones. I remember that name tags on medical personnel became an issue for me at some point. I was always searching for irregularities in them to see who "true" Mount Sinai staff were, and who were not.

I also had hallucinations that were not related to the hospital at all. Around the time of the boutique hallucination, I was in a little gas station store, which sat beside a road in the middle of a forest, with nothing else around. I walked into the small store and shot the clerk dead for no apparent reason. I panicked. I heard another car pull up. I fled into the back room and hid in a small storage area. The people came in, saw the bloody scene, called the police, and left. I was trying to leave when I heard the sirens. At the same time, a vacuum began to run in the storage room. I unplugged it, and still, it ran. The police didn't come to the back room. I was trapped in there for hours into the night, vacuum running, cowered in the corner waiting for the police to arrest me for murder. I wondered if I would ever get out. There was no window or door where I was. The only exit was the front door of the store. There was no escape. Then suddenly I was out, running into the forest. But the story wasn't over. I was a fugitive of justice, forever to be hunted.

It might be rightly asked if some of these weren't just bad dreams and not hallucinations. I don't know. Maybe in some medical appraisal, they were. But for me and my experiences, I draw some distinctions. I've had my share of bad dreams. These were different. These had depth, concreteness, solidness, smell, touch, and sound. They had a dimensionality to them that bad dreams do not. There was a felt-sense to each of them that transcended what I have experienced as dreams. They were a pseudo-reality.

My hallucinations turned dystopian. I think it must have been when I had the tracheostomy that one took place. The country had been politically torn into three camps and three geographic locations. There were those on the far-right, the far-left, and those that were more moderate but generally left-leaning. Three people would be chosen to remotely operate towering leviathan robots on a battlefield. The stakes were high and whatever happened to the machine happened to the operator. I was an operator. One of the other machines in the course of the war ripped into my throat. I tried at one point (perhaps more than one) to rip my trachea tube out. There was a great deal more involved in this hallucination than is told here, but this demonstrates the impact upon the real world of the pseudo-world of hallucination and vice versa. It helps to shape it. Even small comments, or conversations around me, could have a bearing on the hallucination.

Dystopian landscapes began to take over. And I swayed back and forth between these images and what was happening to my body and my surroundings. I can convey only isolated images from them. I haven't forgotten

Delusions, Hallucinations, and Near-Death Experiences

any of the corpus of them, but again, language is unable to apprehend them. Desert vistas in which octopus-looking plants roamed a barren panorama. They were benign, but being hunted to extinction not only for food, which was scarce, but also for pleasure by the ruling class at their bacchanalias, some of which I observed. In another dystopia, mail was difficult to send or receive and everything had a small metal tag attached to it. Receiving stations were set up, and people had to stand in long lines to receive anything. These were only at railroad depots, most of which had dirt floors. The human misery was overwhelming. Guards with assault rifles were everywhere.

Another hallucination had me in the hospital, in a corner, where it was difficult for me to solicit help. Every night people left, and I felt like I was alone for the night. I was told on multiple occasions that the manager wasn't going to let me stay forever. I couldn't move. I was helpless. I was afraid I was going to be thrown out at any moment. Then what? How would I cope on the streets of New York City, in a hospital gown, unable to walk or talk, needing crucial care to survive? Each day morphed into another night of fear and anxiety. I often felt like I was drowning in my sheets so much fluid had been lost. And finally, I was thrown out, in a huge pile of sheets that were soaked and that I was sinking into, unable to struggle to free myself. Eventually, a group from the religious community took me in, but they were illegally occupying the run-down, rat-infested space they had co-opted in an alley in the city. We were able to travel in that hovel as well Strange little creatures like dogs but not quite dogs roamed about. They were a troupe of players, so they went about doing shows.

There were wild, even profligate experiences that involved my classis, the local group of churches in my denomination. It's odd to me that they played such a significant role in my hallucinations, but they did. In these hallucinations another concept kept coming forward: Will-o'-the-wisp. The Will-o'-the-wisp is a phenomenon in folklore, usually associated with the spirit world, ghosts, or other paranormal activity. They actually do exist although they are largely now explained by science. Sometimes they are swamp gases, or auto headlights, such as the case in Paulding, Michigan, in the Upper Peninsula. The folktale that surrounds the Paulding light involves a railroad brakeman who was waving a lantern to warn of a collision when he was struck by the train. Will-o'-the-wisp was a phenomenon of which I had heard, but I can't ever remember discussing it with anyone, nor even using the term, and if I did, it had to have been decades in my past. It struck me as bizarre that this term and sign should be a part of my world of hallucination. In at least two instances, it appeared in a note with the signature being "Will-o'-the-wisp." On only one occasion did I see the phenomenon itself.

In yet another hallucination, I had transferred myself into someone else's body, but it was nothing more than a stick-like figure with a small burlap bag hanging where the heart would be. But it grew. Within the underground religious community at Mount Sinai, I had become something of a leading figure by no choice of my own. Often, I was simply on display. But my very existence in this form was repugnant to others who sought my demise. I had many experiences in this form, and in this form the most surreal of my pseudo-reality events took place. Some of my time there was tracking my family, who had to seek shelter in my dystopian world within the home of one of the families belonging to this freakish cult. My family was among the most extreme practitioners of the group. They offered some safety, but they would quickly turn out, or turn in, anyone that was deemed as dangerous to them. I was particularly worried about how my daughters would survive in such strange environs.

Memories of all these things exist in my mind and in my feelings to the present. Relationships went on in my pseudo-reality. I freeze up at times thinking of events, objects, and the terror that would reign within me, trying to navigate the impossible situations that my mind constructed. The smells and sounds are still with me. One hallucination would branch off into another. What the mind can imagine and what it can conjure out of nothing is a wondrous and horrendous marvel to me.

Not all hallucinations were horrific, though. Some offered respite and beauty. There was a place in a forest where there were wooden stairs in a hill. Beside these stairs, in the hill itself, was a wooden bookcase, rotting, moss-covered, with a few beautifully bound but decaying books that were scattered haphazardly upon the shelves. They contained herbal medical knowledge that only a few of the nurses remembered, recipes for poultices and treatments for pain. There was at the top of this hill in the forest a small bistro. I only stood in the first quaint room of this place, but I liked it. The entry was welcoming and charming and two steps down to the left was a place to sit, only two or three tables. Always just me and whatever guest was with me, and there were a few different ones. There was also a room straight ahead from the entry, but I was never allowed back there. I wonder.

So-called near-death experiences are labeled rightly I believe. As a theologian, I have read a few accounts. These are especially popular in the

Delusions, Hallucinations, and Near-Death Experiences

spiritualist and new age movements, but serious parapsychologists, such as those at the Koestler Center of Edinburgh University, also study this phenomenon. Many Christians also have an appetite for these. This last group is the one that is of concern to me, in part because I believe what they are conveying are hallucinogenic constructs related to a strong belief system, rather than real near-death experiences.

My understanding now arises from two things: first my theological training and second my experience. I say that near-death experiences are thus labeled because they are just that, near death, not death. Many accounts that circulate in the popular culture of Christianity seem to be more like hallucinogenic experiences rather than heavenly revelations. I state this in part because I see in them a great deal of belief confirmation. I think it would be a grave mistake if these experiences are not thoughtfully reflected upon and subjected to a great deal of skepticism. Perhaps what these people experienced was real. This I cannot pass judgment upon. But, perhaps what was experienced was a powerful pseudo-reality created by the magnificent faculties of the mind. That is, if one is fortunate enough to create a world that confirms everything they hold as dear, then they are perhaps in the best space to heal. In either case, near-death experiences do, in my opinion, surpass delusions and hallucinations. They are a different phenomenon that carry features of both while standing in distinction from them. Here, words end as they fail to apprehend what exists in this murky, marvelous, and mysterious Sheol.

I think at three distinct times in my experience, hallucinations gave way to near-death experiences: at the time of my coma, my cardiac arrest during the second transplant, and once when I was on the ventilator and the warning sound was going. In each, I felt myself start slipping away. My experiences also need to be taken with a robust critical eye, but I want to relay them nevertheless. Death is a shared phenomenon of being human, and yet a frontier that is unknown. Perhaps my recollections will add some understanding. But again, near death is not death. I think if someone has this experience that they haven't died, they haven't fully penetrated to the place where the Apostle Paul was given a glimpse. To put it in the words from *The Princess Bride*, people with near-death experiences aren't dead, they're only "mostly dead."

In one near-death experience, I was standing in front of the parsonage at St. John's looking west. The landscape was altered and there was some sort of large retaining wall across the street. There was a steel rail driven into the ground related to another part of this experience or perhaps a hallucination. Then in a moment, in a colossal burst, a black vortex opened and everything from my past shot out at me with a momentum that shocked and consumed me. Then items from that past came, and I was left to reckon with them.

In another, I was watching a beautiful water ballet with music so transcendent that the experience was just auditory but touched my being at its core. I felt that I was surrounded not by heaven, but perhaps some Elysium. I sensed it was a borderland, but a beautiful one. In my hallucinations, I had been in many borderlands that were horrible and hostile, so this stood out as distinct and different.

But it is the final one that strikes me as most likely to be a true near-death experience, an authentic point of choice between living on earth or passing from the borderland into some deeper, purer form of life. Here I was standing in a forest, on a path, solitary, a peaceful loneliness. In front of me in the forest was a small building with a large glass window in the front. It was all congruous with the surroundings, like it belonged. Inside was a woman in spirit form. She was working with what I understood to be a volatile bleach, preparing a garment whose whiteness was beyond compare. I felt it was for me. To my right down the path in the distance, a soft, elegant, comforting pale green light was beckoning me to continue down the path. I felt it was another image of the Will-o'-the-wisp. But then, a thought struck me, perhaps the Will-o'-the-wisp that had been a constant companion to me was the Holy Spirit. This is where I think my theological convictions may have shaped my near-death experience.

Then there was that choice to walk down the path. I felt freedom from my pain, my suffering, all the fear and anxiety that attended me, and the seemingly endless days in the hospital. I was so tired of every movement I had being painful. I was so tired of everything. I was exhausted by my daily battle for life. Then the soft green light, with its promise. The garment was unstained by fluid, urine, and feces. I longed for that light. But then, there was my family, my friends, the communities of faith that had stood with me, prayed for me, and hoped for my return. I turned away from that light, glowing with love and comfort, and I awoke to pain and anguish, and more days of seconds filled with eternities that stretched beyond my ability to see. I awoke again to the promise of agony and affliction. I awoke and I was in the middle of the inconceivable notion of engaging in battle again, with no strength, no resource, only a tattered will, and perhaps the hidden grace of God.

5

Nancy, My Rock Star

A capable wife who can find? She is far more precious than jewels. The heart of her husband trusts in her, and he will have no lack of gain.

—Proverbs—

On a beautiful, normal, peaceful morning in the Hudson Valley, I was drinking coffee, standing at the kitchen counter. I was just about ready to walk over to the church office next door. The peace was broken when a young woman whom I did not know burst into my kitchen from the garage door entrance and in a panicked and raised voice began beckoning me to come with her. "Hurry, come on!" she pulled on the sleeve of my sports coat. "What's going on?" I queried. Thirty minutes later I found myself standing and slipping in a pool of Nancy's blood. We were in the emergency room at Northern Dutchess Hospital. She had lost considerable amounts of blood.

While I was drinking my coffee that morning, Nancy left for her usual morning jog. During that everyday normal activity, she encountered two Cane Corso dogs that had gotten loose and were looking for a victim. They found one in my beautiful Nancy. The name *Cane Corso* in Latin means "bodyguard dog." The breed dates to ancient Greece, and it was a dog that was used in World War I to navigate and engage in trench warfare. They can run 38 miles per hour and have a bite force of 700 pounds per square inch, higher than that of a lion. They have reputedly been used by the Mafia and are sometimes called "Mafia dogs." The ones Nancy encountered were a mating pair: one weighing in at 150 pounds, the other at 100. These dogs belonged to the young woman who had burst into our kitchen that day.

During Nancy's jog, these dogs coordinated an attack on her. The larger one head-butted her to the street, and both dogs began to maul her. Her legs were first. They tore out large sections of her leg muscle. In all, they would bite 14 different places on her body, including both legs and arms and her face. Fortunately, the bites to her head and face were minimized by her hoodie, still loosely tied at her chin though the baseball cap underneath that her ponytail had been threaded through was found later on the side of the road by a friend who lived down the street from where the attack occurred. The owner of the dogs arrived just as the second dog was going again for her face. She quickly called them off, put the dogs in her car, and told Nancy to get in so she could get her to help. Nancy wisely refused to get in the car with the dogs and told her to take the dogs away and then come back and get her. Nancy was losing blood, in shock and pain, struggling up a deserted country road, wondering if that owner would return. She did and brought Nancy to the parsonage. I went out to the driveway and saw Nancy. I vividly recall the scared and puzzled look on her face.

I didn't realize the extent of what had happened. A towel wrapped around her leg and her winter running outfit hid the depth and severity of the wounds. She just wanted to get to the hospital—fast! She feared bleeding to death. We were on our way for the twenty-minute drive. She called 911 while I was driving. When we got to the hospital, I ran into the emergency room and started barking orders. Soon Nancy was in a room, IV in her arm, painkillers in her system, doctors and nurses trying to stem the bleeding. An orderly asked if we minded if he mopped up the blood so no one would slip. A New York State Trooper showed up to get a statement. I stepped out to give it. We had to get pictures. The hospital didn't have a camera. I think everyone involved was in a bit of shock. I called my friend and administrator at St. John's, Shari Juranic, who came and took pictures of the gruesome torn flesh. I am trained to maintain a calm and "in control" demeanor in a crisis. I had my "minister's face" on, but I was scared. I was afraid we were going to lose her. They rushed her by ambulance to the trauma center at Albany Medical Center, about an hour away, because she needed more care than our local hospital could supply.

I got the kids and drove to meet her. It was serious. I went from standing in a pool of blood to standing in the waiting room with my kids. Waiting for hours as doctors in the operating room tried to patch her back together, more than a hundred stitches just below her knees with no stitches at all at some of the worst places. As each hour passed, I grew more concerned—my thoughts went to what life would be like without her. It was impossible, unthinkable, incomprehensible.

When the surgeon finally did arrive to update us, she first related, to my relief, that Nancy would recover with perhaps some nerve damage and/or loss of limb function. She also said that if it had been a child or older person, or if Nancy had been left with the dogs thirty seconds longer, this encounter would have ended in the morgue. After a week in the trauma unit, we brought Nancy home. I and the kids nursed her. It took many visits to the wound care specialist and a full four months before the skin on the back of her leg closed. She had physical therapy for more than a year, determined as she was to run again. And she does. She is simply amazing. I nursed her for a short time. She would nurse me for much longer.

We have both almost lost each other to the hand of death. Yet, we are still here. It is a terrible thing to watch and think: "I may lose the one I love." It is worse, far beyond this, to actually suffer that loss. I know that day will come when one of us is left behind wondering what life will now look like. I believe without reservation that had I lost Nancy that day in 2015, I would not have made it through my ordeal later. There is much more to Nancy's story, and I hope someday that she tells it.

Nancy, her name means *grace*. Nancy lives into her name. I think about the Nancy in Dicken's *Oliver Twist*. Certainly, my Nancy isn't the hardcore vice-ridden character in the novel, but there is one thing they do have in common. Nancy in the novel, for all her faults, sacrifices her life to protect Oliver. Nancy wanted to be my donor. She wanted to make that sacrifice, but she couldn't. Nancy has always protected me, though. There are a lot of slings and arrows and pitfalls that attend life in ministry, and throughout it all, Nancy has been fierce in her protection of me, even when this was a sacrifice for her. Her grace has hovered over me.

Nancy is a sweet, kind person. Always has a smile, a joy in her heart that no one can steal, a certainty about her faith—titanium-like—and a kindness that is accompanied by fidelity. She has beautiful eyes full of love. Sometimes though, I see the care of life she carries when I look into those eyes, and I want to reach in and wipe it away. She loves adventure. She loves her family and is constantly about taking care of every one of us, attending to the mundane details with which no one else wants to be bothered. She is soft but ever so resilient, absolutely unbreakable. She carries dreams with her too, and often the rest of us are so inwardly bent that we don't see them.

During my eight-month stay, Nancy made dozens of long trips from Red Hook to Manhattan, a drive of about 100 miles that took two to three hours each way, depending on traffic. She stayed for most of the first four months in a small room in East Harlem at the Transplant Living Center of Mount Sinai. She spent hundreds of hours by my bedside. She had to juggle so many things other than me and my situation. All manner of things came at her.

At the worst low of my situation, when I had gone into a coma, she had to tend to my mother as well, and this was no mean feat. My mom suffers from Alzheimer's and had been living with us for six years. As I hovered between life and death, it was apparent my mother needed more care and supervision than could be provided safely at home, especially now that Nancy was no longer there to watch over her. So, Nancy had to do all the work to place her in a care facility. In fact, she was touring the nursing home the day I was first offered organs.

On top of this, both Penelope and Valerie were dealing not only with the real possibility of losing their father but also their own very serious life traumas. Nancy had to drive to Chicago with Penelope to retrieve her belongings that had been left after a truncated first semester at a college there. It was at a noisy restaurant on that trip that she learned from a doctor that I would need a second transplant. One could not have devised a better stratagem to "take out" a family that deeply loved each other than this. It was brutal, surreal, and relentless, and Nancy was managing this.

At the same time, she came and sat calmly by my side for those horrible, unpromising hours. She watched as I slipped in my mind, in my body, and in my spirit. She watched as I faded day after day into nothing more than a skeleton, a mummy staring at the ceiling. She sat. She prayed. And she believed. I think until truly all other belief around her was probably pro forma, an attempt to comfort her. I don't think for a moment that Nancy wasn't shaken or didn't have thoughts about my loss. It's simply that until I was in fact dead, her belief also was not dead. That's who she is. As our family chaplain (that's what I call this minister colleague now) Kendra said: "Nancy is a rock star." True enough. But this rock star wasn't prancing up and down a stage to the adulation of crowds. No, this rock star waded deep into life's swamp, handled all its unbearable vagaries together with mounds of its paperwork, and sat by my bed, while managing a household and caring for other people, including how, when, and what she communicated to our church, to minister to them amid this ever-growing crisis.

When she was at my bedside, I felt more secure, far less anxious, and reassured. When I saw her eyes, I saw love. She could mediate and advocate while she was there, too. But mostly, the comforting memory I have of her was her sitting quietly sewing her needlepoint and just being there. Nothing more powerful in my world existed. Nothing anchored me better. We harness vast powers as creatures. Still, it escapes us that those things that most would deem mundane, unimportant, or irrelevant altogether are the very forces that God in divine sovereignty chooses, as if in a laugh God says, "O, you don't want that? Okay, I'll take it then."

I marvel to this day that such a person as Nancy exists and marvel even more that God has put her in my life to begin with. She's a rock star. She is prancing on a stage, rockin' out, but like there's only an audience of one, and I suppose that's right. There's an audience of one. It is a good fortune to the world that that audience isn't me: it's God.

There is a quiet, beautiful way in which Nancy flows through life, even in the ways she must battle with it at times. She doesn't bring offense; she demurs. Her presence is a hospitality to others. Yet, her inner strength is without rival. It takes a lot of strength to pull yourself up from the pavement and limp down a rural road with no help in sight if your legs have been shredded. She did that. It takes a lot to move across the ocean, young children in tow, and live in a country that has visible and invisible signs of the aftermath of war still present. She did that.

It takes a lot to sit for hours on end in a hospital chair doing needlepoint while someone you love dies in front of your eyes. She did that. The Apostle Paul has it right: love endures all things. Love is this amazingly fragile thing; it can shatter so easily. But love, its essence, survives. The fires of love may die out here and there, but love itself endures all things. It does not die. In Christianity, we say this is so because as the Apostle John says: God *is* love. Because God endures, love, which is constituent of God, endures.

In our liturgy of marriage in the Reformed Church in America, there is a fantastic statement made by the celebrant: "Human commitment is fragile and human love imperfect, but the promise of God is eternal, and the love of God can bring our love to perfection." So many marriages end broken because they ultimately try to go it alone, that is, with only human commitment and love. Nancy has always leaned into God's promise and

God's love, and when all my humanity is hanging out like hashtags on a military uniform, our human love becomes fortified because she lives in God's love.

Love has ways in which it is known. Love is known for its humility, kindness, meekness, and forgiveness. So many marriages are governed by coarseness and hostility so harmony cannot be found there. Love also has ways it changes. Unfortunately, some marriages don't survive long enough to allow love to change. Love has a morphology. It deepens over time. Its character strengthens with duration and circumstance. When I officiate weddings, I tell the couple that "where Christ dwells, the infinite character of love dwells." Nancy dwells in Christ, and so the infinite character of love dwells with her. She brings that to our marriage.

When a doctor says to you: "We're doing everything we can, but we're only human," things are not going well and probably will not end well. Nancy heard those words. Her response was not: "Thank you, doctor, I appreciate all that you are doing for him." Hers was: "That's okay. We've got the rest covered!" I'm not sure what the doctor might have made of that response, but I'm guessing he hadn't heard it before. It's extraordinary faith that uses that kind of language. The faith that Nancy carries with her every day. She carried it even two weeks earlier on December 16, when I said to her, "I need to go over my funeral service with you." When she said okay and took out a paper and pen, I knew at that moment how bleak and serious things had become. She says she did it because of how stubborn I had become. We both also knew that death was a distinct possibility for me. Even then, Nancy's faith was tenacious and unyielding.

When Mount Sinai closed to visitors due to Covid, we were separated for ten long weeks, from the middle of March to the end of May 2020. I was unable to use my hands, so I could not use my phone which meant we were completely out of touch for most of that time. Just five days after our separation started, I had to be returned to the Transplant Intensive Care Unit and put back on the ventilator. Then I began being moved from one floor to another as the hospital tried to deal with the ever-increasing flood of Covid patients.

When I tested positive and began my Covid isolation, my hallucinations taunted me. I needed to understand why Nancy wasn't there anymore, faithfully, quietly there. The loss of Nancy cut me to the core. I knew the hospital was in an upheaval but did not have any idea that Mount Sinai was the epicenter of the pandemic in the States at that time. No one could come, but Nancy, surely, she would be there, somehow, unless something tragic had happened. It occurred to me that given the scope of what was going on, she and my children might have all died in the pandemic. That was my conscious self. My dissociative self told me something different. Either way, Nancy wasn't there, wasn't going to be there anymore for me. My protector, the grace in my life, the love that would never leave, had left. This was all I knew. And if Nancy was gone, so was my heart. Not only was my mind breaking apart, but my heart now, too, knew pain. The pain that had plagued my body now ravaged my heart. Nancy was gone. If my hallucination were true and she had left me for another man, then at least the children would still have her. If she had passed in the pandemic, then I had no way to get to the children. They would be left alone in the world. Yes, they were adults but still getting their footing in life. Either way, I had lost her, and another part of me died. There was nothing to say but that divine judgment was now intermingled with divine indifference or divine cruelty.

Days went on like this in my mind, and the helplessness and hopelessness of my situation were magnified as never before. It was a great day when I found that she was alive and talking with me: not mad, not left, and not dead. My love lived! Jeri and I talked about how great this was, that in our isolation, something good, something promising arose in the darkness. Nancy still loved me. She just couldn't come because of the pandemic. I thought I might have lost her this second time. But in neither case did God see fit to remove Nancy, this wonderful covering of grace in my life.

Falling asleep next to Nancy when I finally returned home was such a wonderful thing. One morning after I awoke, I slowly made my way downstairs and into the kitchen. I had my coffee and breakfast. This alone was enough to fatigue me. When I returned to the bedroom, I sat on the sofa and looked at the surface next to me. It was stacked with papers. As I looked through them, it dawned on me. These were artifacts from Nancy's time while I was at Mount Sinai. Menus from Manhattan. Fliers that are handed out on the streets. Receipts for groceries and gas. It struck me that I was handling something sacred, a life of sacrifice of which I knew nothing. Then an epiphany came. Nancy had an entire existence parallel to mine of which I knew nothing. So ill, in such a struggle to survive, I never thought of it. How had life been for her? What did she do? How had she existed? Where did she eat? How was it for her? I handled these artifacts stunned. I wanted to know. In my frail state, I asked her, "How was it for you all those months?" Her answer was brief, something like, "You know, it was hard, challenging." She didn't elaborate, and I didn't push. I'm amazed I made it, and I'm amazed that she made it. For as many days as possible, Nancy was at the hospital at my side. Many nights she walked the blocks back to the Transplant Living Center alone with her burdens and mine. If I didn't have the comfort of home during my time at Mount Sinai, neither did Nancy. It's hard for me to think of what she endured for me.

Of course, my love for Nancy has taken on a new, profound depth, more than I could have imagined. There is a love there, the depths of which cannot be seen. It reaches into the dark parts of me, and so much of Nancy's inner beauty is known only to me. All our time, all our crises, and all our journey have formed this love. It lives in a secret place where we dwell, where two people who love each other have almost lost each other. I know that in a very dark time and place for me, I thought it was gone. And I remember the joy in my house of pain when I learned that it was not.

There is a deep peace that comes with a love that joins two together, so closely, that this love moves in, even when it hurts, even when the cost is high. The two move as one. I think that's Nancy and me. We dwell within each other's shadow. The psalmist says that we dwell in God's shadow—dark, foreboding, comforting. It is also where God's mystery, deep and impenetrable, exists. This is the realm where God's decree and decision—good and bad, hard and horrible—exist. This realm is where we abide. We abide in the realm of God's shadow. Each of us casts a shadow. Certainly, the physical phenomenon is known to us. But we also have a soulish shadow. It too is deep and mysterious, hidden but from an intimate few. It is an area we protect and hide. Nancy and I dwell there, in each other's shadow. She dwells in my shadow in so many ways. She sees who I am and loves me anyway. She sees all the weakness, the hurt, the bad and the good, and loves anyway.

I am so glad that I have more time with Nancy. We have both paid a price for it. When the day is new, seeing her smile, I am glad, and when the night comes, I am grateful for the day that was, with her whose name means grace.

6

Samuel, Valerie, Penelope, and Jack

The soul is healed by being with children.

— FYODOR DOSTOEVSKY —

Like any average father, I love my children to a fault. I loved them as little children, and we had our share of fun, laughter, snuggles, and tears. I love them as adults. They are evidence of the blessing of God toward me. They are all quite different of course, each coming from the same genes, raised by the same parents, and in the same environment. The thing that is unique to them is their experience. Having different experiences means that they learn to respond to external phenomena and stimuli in particular ways.

    Samuel has a calm satirical, philosophical, kind, playful, and logical disposition. Valerie has a sarcastic extroversion, which shelters a sweet vulnerability and reveals a desire for justice. She also has a kind playfulness. Valerie is a survivor and from this comes an understanding of people who have been traumatized. She is courageous, and her name fits her well. She is a person of valor. Penelope, who fits the profile of our only native New Yorker, displays the caution of a gambler. She has underneath that a genuine kindness and concern for people combined with a natural intuitive attentiveness of people and a braveness that defies her petite frame. Jack is Samuel's partner in life. Bright, fun, hardworking, and adventurous, a marvelous addition to our family.

All my kids had to deal in a very real sense with the probability that I would die. As individuals, they naturally coped in different ways. I think grief has as many expressions as there are individuals in the world since grief works through the makeup of each. My experience as a minister has led me to believe, contrary to some psychology models, that grief doesn't follow any set course and is nearly impossible to track. It wanders where it will in the soul of each individual, expressing itself according to the composition of each personality, and of course the nature and depth of the relationship between the deceased and the person.

Through my ordeal, all my children would extend themselves to me with the gift of who they are. They were all there the day I was admitted. They were all allowed to come back and see me before I went into the prep area, where only Nancy was allowed. I was able to say that I loved them, and that moment of being able to say those words was more important than I could have ever imagined. Then my journey began.

✳ ✳ ✳

Music was perhaps the medium that was best suited to reaching my soul when other things failed. Before the Covid pandemic, volunteer singers and musicians would come to my room. Somehow music was always comforting to me. But no instrument, no song touched me as deeply as those Penelope played and sang. She has a wonderful voice and plays a bit of guitar and ukulele. The ukulele was easier to transport so that's what she brought to the hospital on Christmas Day and again on Father's Day. She sang these soft lovely songs to me. Her voice drifted into the hallway, and the staff would comment on how beautiful her voice was. In her voice was love, and I felt that. Penelope sang many songs to me. The ones that she had written meant the most to me. Her songs, her instrument, her voice reached deep into my soul, deep into a broken place that had been shattered into thousands of pieces. It is a remarkable thing that music has its own power to heal beyond medical science. I was broken in so many ways, but her music healed a part of that brokenness.

During my recovery at home, Penelope also sang to me. I asked her to play *The Magnificat*. I struggled to sing along. It was beautiful to hear and to sing. But I also had a strange sensation that there was a gulf between Penelope and me. As if she were keeping her distance. It was like she might not want to risk getting too close because if I regressed, if I died, it would be the same wound reopened. For whatever reason I sensed it was there, and it hurt me. I didn't know what to do. I tried to engage her, but the gambler showed up. This continued until the Christmas after my return home.

At Christmas, we do a Secret Santa thing as a family. Penelope had drawn my name. It was fortuitous grace from God, I think. Penelope wrote me the most beautiful letter. The envelope was handmade and graceful, a time-consuming proposition. I opened it to find numerous things enclosed. The letter was kind, delightful, full of love, full of understanding about how I felt. Penelope is like that, keenly in tune with the hurts and needs of others. In the letter, she wrote: "I get the feeling you've been sad that we don't spend time together. Especially because you've been trying to make up for lost time and all that. So, I figured time was the most valuable gift I could give you." I broke down in tears. Suddenly everything was all right; everything was going to be all right. This gift plumbed the depth of a wound and healed it. Christmas gifts don't usually do that.

Penelope, along with all my family, endured an extended trauma. It was a flight of life from her father. It was watching and thinking about someone who loved her, played games with her, laughed with her, supported her, cheered for her, cherished her, and delighted in her wonderful existence, slowly dying before her. This brings an existential death to the one watching, real and menacing. Life is reordered against the will and in discordance with the heart. There is a certain chaos that erupts. Death separates, and the heart, to survive, must at some point let go. I now understand to a fuller measure what broken-heart syndrome is. The heart begins in its first agonizing steps to make this impossible adjustment. Then it is just as confounding when life defeats death, and the process has to be reversed. I think I understand a bit of what Penelope must have struggled with.

One of the gifts of time that Penelope gave me that Christmas day in 2020 was the gift of music. We did this when I gained better control of my hands and had some strength in my fingers. We both took our guitars, sat in my study, and Penelope and I talked and played. She was teaching me the use of a capo. Slowly, just broken notes here and there, but my daughter and I were again making music together in our lives. When brokenness was present, Penelope reached in to heal me with her gifts. I think we underestimate the power of the gifts we have. Often, we hold them back because we think that they don't have a place, a purpose, or a power to do anything. But they do. They have the power to heal a broken man.

We all have this ability. The power to heal each other. There are wounds of the soul profoundly deep that no scan, no blood test, no biopsy, and no physician can detect. These are the wounds of life: wounds that are self-inflicted and wounds that others inflict, wounds that God inflicts, and the wounds that simply come while we are walking through an average day when average turns into a savage, raging from what are random strikes of fate. In a moment, all our life—all that we knew and loved—is gone, and tomorrows have ceased. Healing comes, but scars remain. We hold the vast powers of healing each other. Sometimes it only takes an act of will met with charity to reach out to another and say in word and deed, "be healed." Whether she was singing in the hospital, or giving a gift on Christmas, Penelope was saying to her broken father: "Be healed." And I was healed.

✻ ✻ ✻

As a little girl, Valerie was sunshine. She loved life. She loved school; she loved playing and laughing. All of this was a perfect cover for the little bits of sweet mischief that would come out on occasion. She was radiant, and so very much fun. This was the girl we took with us to Croatia, where I taught in a Protestant seminary. Croatia was a country recovering from a national trauma and a genocidal war. The marks of this conflict were still on the buildings. All my children walked into Croatian classrooms not knowing the language and most teachers not knowing theirs. They walked into a building riddled with bullet and shell pocks. These were not the cheery American classrooms they were used to. They were stark, unwelcoming.

Valerie's teacher was especially harsh. My beautiful daughter was bright and curious. She was used to a nurturing classroom. She was met with harshness. Her teacher treated her like an idiot. She had very little use for Valerie. She saw it as a personal imposition that Valerie was in her class at all and made everyone around aware of that. The teacher complained constantly to Nancy and to the school administration, which insisted Valerie remain in her class because she was the only third-grade teacher who spoke English. That teacher took all this out on eight-year-old Valerie. Every day that child walked into school was a dizzying trauma. She started drawing to make constructive use of her time as she was neglected. She became an accomplished artist. This is the beauty that emerged from ugly trauma. She also survived a horrible somatic trauma at the hands of her peers in Croatia.

Samuel, Valerie, Penelope, and Jack

I remember climbing into Valerie's bed night after night, to comfort her (and myself), to read to her, and sometimes to hold her as she cried herself to sleep. When she was asleep, I would find a quiet place because then I would weep for my child and for the circumstance I had put her in. I wasn't sure how long we would make it in Croatia with three young children. The personal cost was high, but the cost to my children was much higher. I was pursuing my career; they were plunged into hell. It wasn't all bad, though; there were many happy times and wonderful memories made in Europe. Our kids and our family bonded because of it. Samuel, Valerie and Penelope are the best of siblings and friends.

The return to the States was no easier for them, however. They were met with a culture they did not understand. It was hard for them to find friends. Samuel did his last year and a half of high school in his room in a virtual program he had started overseas. Thankfully, he was able to graduate through that program and keep those long-distance relationships, but ones closer to home were few and far between. The girls were in public school with others their age, but their experiences put them at odds with Americans who had lived sheltered, and in many ways, entitled, lives. Again, they were alienated.

Valerie changed in those years. She is still a wonderful, caring person. She is still laughter and cheer. She is still sunshine. But clouds come now, her softness worn to a cynical edge at times. Life has worn her. Her artistic talent is excellent, and she began her studies at Savannah College of Art and Design. It was a time of promise, and we hoped as parents that this would be a wonderful experience for her. While there were many positives there, she decided to transfer after two years to a school near home. Then she was the victim of a crime. Now more trauma, more hurt.

These traumas were then followed by watching her father pass before her. During much of my time in the hospital, she struggled to find her way. She moved in with friends back in Savannah and then in Chattanooga. It was hard on her, the distance adding to anxiety. Valerie and I are a father and daughter who talk together. At this point in her life, during trauma and then the Covid shutdown, being at a distance took a toll on her. At the point where she needed to talk with her father, I was withering away physically and mentally. Grief is with me to this day over this.

But Valerie, my artist! The one who works with charcoal—ashes—to make beautiful art created another thing of beauty out of rubble. She began writing letters to me. Her handwriting is like art, too, because the Croatians still put value into making beautiful script. She worked through her struggles, and things she wanted to say to me, and pleaded for guidance from a father who could not even breathe on his own let alone speak. She shared deep things, troubling things, and poignant things. In sum, there were twenty-five lengthy letters from her to me while I was in the hospital. When I now read them, to this day my heart breaks, and yet my spirit rejoices.

I was a long way from emerging into any sort of stable condition on February 5, 2020, when Valerie wrote as she was struggling for direction for her future:

> Dad, you know me better than anyone I think . . . you've seen me through everything that has happened to me. I need your advice on what direction I should head in. Most of the time I think that you would surely say that you believe I should go fully into the world of art; find a studio somewhere and sell my work independently. But when I think about that I think of how it would feel so empty without you.

A few days later, on February 12, she wrote: "It's been one hundred and twelve days since the last time I hugged you. I miss you. You should come to visit me in Savannah. I'll try to write to you again soon, Dad. I love you, and I miss you terribly." February marked a particularly horrible time for me, coming around from a second transplant that I didn't even remember happening, dealing with a trachea tube in my neck I never understood. This was the month in which I was exhausted in my body, in my spirit, and in my mind. The struggle seemed insurmountable for me, and I did in so many ways just want the pain and suffering to stop. I had had enough.

Both Nancy and Valerie knew that my will and my spirit were failing along with my body. After one of her visits, Nancy and Valerie were discussing the situation. Valerie relayed part of this in her letter: "I told Mom after one of our visits, 'I just . . . don't think he wants it.' I would tell Mom, and she would put her hand over her mouth and nod in agreement. It's been hard" (Feb. 25). At the end of that same letter, she said: "For the most part throughout my life, no matter how depressed you might have been or how sick, I had this unprecedented confidence that our conversations would never end." She ended the letter: "What's so terrifying is I have the feeling I might not have another conversation with you." Valerie knows now in concrete ways that a tomorrow will come when no more conversations will happen. I know that, too. But perhaps the most powerful and poignant letter was written on February 24:

> Since you've been in the hospital, I've spent a lot of time thinking about the possibility that maybe you don't ever end up leaving the hospital, maybe you don't make it. Maybe you never get to see me graduate from college, or get married or have a baby, or succeed and excel in my career. Maybe all of that is something that we won't experience together. So I've wrestled quite a bit with this concept that you might die sometime soon. And it's agonizing and awful and horrifying—but there is something else. A little bit of relief at the thought that you wouldn't have to be in pain anymore.

In that same letter, she writes about her own mortality. Valerie thought that my passing first might make the thought of her own mortality less intimidating and not more. That perhaps I'd be waiting for her. She asked me if I felt that about my dad's passing a little more than a year before. I have never been frightened by death itself. However, I have had dread about having a prolonged period of suffering and isolation before I died. I was right to be afraid of those things. I've lived through it, and it was more terrifying than I could have imagined in this fertile mind of mine. My dad went through that, too, before he died. I hope to see him, too. I need to speak with him now, but there are, for the time being, no more conversations to be had between us.

Nevertheless, I did survive, yet death still awaits me. So, too, does resurrection. It is said that Jesus' wounds are eternal in nature but that ours are transitory. The first is a matter of my faith, and I hold it still. The second, however, I think is not true. This life, our wounds—although I hold, too, that they will be healed—are still a part of our constitution. I live through what I live through. It is a part of who I am. Frankly, as odd as it may seem, I don't want to lose that part of me. Like Jesus, I hope to have a new body made from the seed (as the Apostle Paul puts it) of what I am now. I don't wish for the pain of the wound in the least, but I get the scar. I get to keep the memory of the battle I survived. I recall hearing that a rabbi was once asked why God created humanity at all. His response was "Because God loves a good story." I think all great works of literature are reduced to a single theme in the end: redemption or the lack thereof.

In my earthly existence, I am an expression of this redemption. I was able to be at Valerie's college graduation. She had a long and hard road to get there. I was with her on that day in New Hampshire. I hope to see her get married. I think of the day when Valerie places her child in my arms. I envision myself saying the same thing the old Simeon said when he beheld Christ as an infant. On that day (although I hope I have many more after that) I think I can say: "Let now your servant depart in peace." I would have a peace about it all. I would long for the same for all my children and their children. Still, someday there will be no tomorrow.

For now, I am able to see my child, Valerie, on a more or less weekly basis. We hug—usually long hugs—and we will sometimes whisper "I'm glad I'm here; I'm glad I can hold you" or something along those lines. Someday it will not be a hundred and twenty-odd days from our last hug. Someday there will be no tomorrow for us, and the gulf of eternity will stand between us. If there is anything I could wish for then, it would be that future day, when Valerie, an old woman, will cross into the eternal, made young. I will be there, arms open wide. We will embrace, and we will say: "I'm glad you're here. It seems like only yesterday that we last hugged each other." Then, and from then on, there will only be the promise of tomorrows.

✻ ✻ ✻

Samuel is our firstborn. We had wanted a child, but he was delayed in getting to us for ten years. In those ten years, we prayed, and others prayed. He came almost at the moment when I had finally decided to pursue ordination in the Reformed Church in America, a decision that was also delayed. It was the very day I met with my student supervisor about the process that I received news from Nancy that Samuel was on the way. At the end of his crib, Nancy taped a sign: "For this child I prayed" (1 Sam 1:27). It was only natural that we should name him Samuel, meaning *God has heard*. During this process of finishing the necessary time and criteria for ordination, I was called as a youth pastor and eventually associate pastor at a church in Long Beach, California. Samuel was still a baby when we arrived there.

He was a curious child, focused, intent to the exclusion of all else on whatever he was interested in. He loved electronic and mechanical things, and even wanted to build a car—"a real one, not a model!" He didn't like being pulled away from things, which led sometimes to mercurial episodes. We found that we needed to give him notices before we transitioned or went somewhere. I remember on more than one occasion that I needed to put him in a position where I could restrain him and comfort him all at once. He was strong as a toddler and preadolescent to be sure. As I would restrain and rock him, I would say in a calm voice, "Be the calm." He later told me he didn't understand that until he grew older, but at some level, he knew what it meant. Yet, he was marvelous, such an exceptionally gifted child. I would say even magnificent.

We seemed always to be playing and laughing. He would look with wonder at every discovery life brought him. He loved the trampoline we had in Long Beach, and we brought it to Fishkill, New York, when we moved for me to take another ministerial position. I think he liked the freedom it gave to him. The trampoline wasn't just about bouncing. It was about joy and freedom and times together and family gatherings as we all climbed on together and even had picnics on it. We would eventually have to leave that trampoline behind as we prepared to move to Croatia. I know this was a heart-breaking loss of a love for Samuel. It was a loss for all of us.

I loved Samuel as a child. I love him for the man he has become. As an adult, Samuel is a kind, beautiful, caring person; he is the calm. He loves books and philosophy and is something of an expert in Søren Kierkegaard, the Danish theologian and philosopher. While we were in Croatia, Samuel, like Valerie and Penelope, went to the local public school. Not understanding the language was his first big hurdle. His teachers treating him as a non-entity was another. This must have been a tremendous shift for Samuel, the much-anticipated first child who was used to being the center of attention. But he learned the language: he became close to being a native speaker. His regional Slavonian accent led people, when we traveled to the coast of Croatia, to place him in that region simply by the nativeness of his speech. His mind was always active; never did his curiosity abate. Even when the school failed him, he read the encyclopedia that we had taken with us. We eventually pulled Samuel out of the school system to home-school him. He and I read novels together each night. The last novel I remember reading to Samuel was *Ivanhoe*. He followed along with intensity and fascination. I taught him what I knew about chess, and we got him a chess program that he spent hours on. He developed a real love for this game, which is an art as well as a sport.

As he grew, he began to learn more about what I did and what I taught at the seminary in Croatia. He started to love philosophy. He was always filled with probing questions that had depth. I think the only thing that saved me in that respect was my many years of education. He learned that each question he was asking had many viewpoints and only led to more questions, and this he loved. He has never stopped having those questions, big questions, questions about life and ethics, serious and life-impacting questions. He is a seeker of truth, and for this, I rejoice. He eventually went on to college and then earned a master's degree in information and library science. He now works as a librarian at Princeton University, a perfect place for him. He is a considered, peaceful man.

Samuel and I have always been close. We have a father-son relationship that I think would be envied by many. He shares with me a love of books, a good philosophical discussion, and a good game of chess. It is uncomplicated, and we have so many mutual loves that we understand each other. He is still playful and sports a wonderful sense of humor. He cares for others: he cares for the earth and all of creation. This child, who we sometimes wondered whether he would outgrow his intense focus and periods of mercurialness, has emerged as a beautiful person. He and his partner Jack are lovers of nature, something that he never lost from his childhood. They are both minimalists, careful and considered. Samuel, as serious a thinker as he is, has never lost the playfulness of his childhood, and laughter comes easily to those around him.

I can't say how Samuel was feeling about my situation or that I was close to dying. He keeps that sort of thing close to the heart. I do know in the face of the worst of it, he and Valerie were still able to find some levity for relief. Mostly riffing off lines from a family favorite, *The Princess Bride*: "Life is pain, Highness. Anyone who says differently is selling something." "He is only mostly dead. See, mostly dead is still slightly alive." "Look he moved his finger, isn't that marvelous?" I did ask him at one point what was going through his head when he was facing the prospect of losing me. He said that he was talking with Valerie about it and just said, "I guess he's not coming back." That is a heavy realization, simply looking it straight in the face and stating the reality of it all.

He found a real blessing in Jack, his spouse. The two of them lived with us for two years, a real gift to allow us, the parents and siblings, to get to know Jack as the two had met in college in Michigan. Jack is the organizer, the detail person in this couple, the one who naturally made the arrangements for a bed and breakfast for the four of them to stay near the hospital when I was first admitted.

Jack wrote to me a few times. In one correspondence they shared about mystery, about its profundity, and its nature. They also shared about the pitfalls of quick, unreflective answers in the face of mystery and how this robs God. Better to keep silent and to reflect on mystery's presence. What wonderful words for my circumstance. Jack is a student at Princeton Theological Seminary and has preached on several occasions at St. John's.

These words hit me with all that pastoral care should be, and with the feeling that my child-in-law might lose me, and they and I are close, too. Jack, in the letter, spoke of something else: my future, our future, and the dreams that our family has together shared.

Samuel had another role to play, but this was after my release from Mount Sinai. A veil of fog coated my mind for a long time, both in the hospital and after my return home. Thinking clearly, making decisions, and having confidence in the choices I made were difficult. Simple things like remembering directions to a common destination could be challenging. Trusting my moves and negotiating my way through life were skills I once had and needed to cultivate again. As I said, Samuel and I played chess when he was a boy. He loved the game and became proficient enough that one day I met the surprise that I had given to my father when I was a boy playing chess—a loss. He studied it. He understands the game and has an intuition for it that is necessary to its mastery. He also plays a great deal with his friends and colleagues and, of course, online now.

Because of my mind fog (either from Covid or my long and complicated hospital stay), my doctor recommended that I begin playing chess again, and so I did with Samuel. Most of the time we play online since we live in different states. In the beginning, it was a challenge for me to survive very many moves. Slowly I began to survive more moves and more. That was what I worked toward, not a win, just prolonged survival, and deeper concentration. It was a good barometer because I could tell when I missed something easy, hadn't considered moves, or caught dangers that were apparent when I replayed the games. I bought chess books (too many!), immersed myself in the game, and solved hundreds of puzzles online. It helped, and the mists of befuddlement began to retreat. Loss after loss sure, but I was empirically surviving deeper into the game. Then the marvelous day came, and I finally won a game. Samuel isn't the kind of person to let someone win, not even dear old Dad. No, on that day, months upon months after leaving Mount Sinai, I triumphed on the field of sixty-four in the most complex game known to humanity. I remember that day, not so much because I won, but because Samuel and I had spent that time together even though we were so far away from one another. Samuel helped heal my mind.

While I have lost many things as a result of my ordeal, I have also gained some things. One is that as I play Samuel, I am with Samuel in a sense even when we are far apart. I set up the pieces on a beautiful chess table in which I indulged as a self-gift for surviving through the suffering. As we play online, I transfer the moves to the board. It's the best I get when I can't have him there with me. As I look at the board, I can see that wonderful mind of his working. He is with me, in the same way Penelope is when I read her beautiful books or watch her music videos on TikTok, or see Valerie's masterful art.

My children, now adults, are remarkable individuals. They all played a major role in keeping me alive and in making me well. A father can ask no more of his children than that they grow to be caring and kind people who make the world a better place. I have that. They are a gift to me and everyone around them. I understand why Scripture refers to children in terms of prosperity. It is wealth by which one is blessed by their presence in the world. I am wealthy beyond measure because they are in mine. I am blessed that I have more time with them, time to love and laugh, time to talk and play. This is something for which I am consciously grateful. But I am also conscious of another thing more than ever before. Someday there will be no tomorrow, and our time together on earth will have passed.

7

When Hope Unborn Had Died

*Let me tell you something my friend. Hope is a dangerous thing.
Hope can drive a man insane.*

—RED IN *THE SHAWSHANK REDEMPTION*—

Red says these things to his friend, Andy, in Stephen King's novella *Rita Hayworth and Shawshank Redemption*. In the movie adaptation, he says it to Andy after Andy is released from isolation in "the hole." Andy says that hope was never lost because he could turn his mind to other things, like Mozart.

I have had many struggles in my life. I have even lost hope. But losing hope is different than experiencing the death of hope inside of you. It's an awful death to experience. It is a darkness that envelops you, creeps in, and extinguishes light. This darkness strangled life, and it assassinated my will. My defensive mechanisms shut down. I had no capacity to fight, and nothing in the future seemed even remotely possible to achieve. When the death of hope comes, it sweeps in, guts, and eradicates all embers that glow with the prospect that something better might emerge on the horizon.

By force of will, I opened to the possibility of hope at one point during my sojourn at Mount Sinai. I saw a glimmer of hope's shadowy specter flash like a small flake of gold in a Western riverbed. I lived to regret it. It was pyrite, fool's gold. You see, hope is a dangerous thing with which to play. Hope, when it is overcome by the *tohu va vohu* (that is the chaos and nothingness of the uncreated at the beginning of Genesis), is a mutilated horror.

I arrived at a place in my odyssey when hope was asphyxiated and murdered by something daemonic, uncreated, unreal-yet-real. Emerging from this was an unformed but palpable "not-hope," that is, the complete and true death of hope. Once or twice, I saw a brief twinkle, grabbed for it, and it was gone. "Not-hope" sardonically laughing, menacingly taunting. The Apostle John says in the book of Revelation: "I looked and there was a pale green horse! Its rider's name was Death, and Hades followed with him" (Rev 6:8a). The rider of the pale horse had ridden through the vestiges of my hope and left the landscape bare. The winds of my soul echoed with his howling. My soul and body were a wasteland.

The worst came in the spring. In March, less than a week after the hospital shut down to visitors due to Covid, I had to go back to the Transplant Intensive Care Unit and back on the ventilator. Later, all the transplant patients in the Intensive Care Unit were moved to a space designated for recovery from surgery, not designed for conscious patients. This was so desperate Covid patients could be placed on our floor, where the critical would be separated from each other in rooms that could be easily monitored by staff.

We were in a small space, ward-like, like an old war movie. The only thing that separated us were curtains. I could see fellow patients opposite me. Mount Sinai was still in the early stages of "the siege," as it was to become known. I had been informed by doctors from the Infectious Disease department that I did not have Covid. I didn't know then what that was, but if it was something I didn't have, I was grateful. At this point I was beginning my long recovery from my second transplant surgery and had had so many infections, not having something was encouraging. I was with other patients. I was placed right in front of the staff station, and I was being cared for.

Physical therapy started coming at that time. I was able to get up, sit in a chair (which was a painful ordeal), and briefly walk around the small ward with my walker. Occupational therapy also worked with me at that time. I was told in April that they were getting ready to transfer me to acute physical therapy. I knew this meant something. Something big, something impossible. If I could get to acute care, it was the brass ring. It meant I would most certainly be released in less than a month. I was getting closer to the dream of home. I began to think something different and better might be on the horizon. It was days before my transfer to acute rehabilitation was to happen and just as I was ready to birth hope in my soul even amid hallucinations. It was then when I had nursed that ember of hope to life, the siege and its indiscriminate savageness and cruelty came; the pale green horse and its ghastly rider met that ember and swept me away, with certain death ahead of me.

On April 30, when release was so very close, I was diagnosed with Covid while staying in that non-Covid unit. I was later told that my neighboring patient had had a false negative test and had passed it on to me. I was rushed out immediately and placed in isolation. Now, not only were visitors restricted, but I also had very little contact with staff as they were strictly limited in the amount of time they could be in the room. *Brave*, *heroic*, and *valorous* are the words that come to mind when I think of all the staff that still attended to me and my many needs.

What awaited me in my isolation room was a large, noisy, negative-pressure ventilation unit and a boarded-up window, where it had been hastily installed. Between the room ventilator and the personal protective equipment that the staff had to wear, it became all but impossible for me to hear them or they me. The persistent drone of the ventilation unit was an auditory torture. Unbeknownst to any of us, my hearing had begun to fail, due largely, I later learned, to massive amounts of antibiotics used to keep me alive in the earlier, critical days after the second transplant. But it was that ventilator that first made me aware of it. I was alone. I was in isolation for six weeks. I was in "the hole." I had done a dangerous thing: I had courted hope. Isolation and hope are a bad mix. They can drive a man insane. Hope died in me; its ashes scattered over the ravaged battlefield of my soul.

During this time in isolation, I was moved a few times. Once I was told I was going to a room with a window. I hadn't looked through a window since December 30. There were windows in the Transplant Intensive Care Unit, but due to my critical state there, I was unable to look out of them though I could get the benefit of sunshine there. My bed turned the corner as it was wheeled into this new room. I saw it: the ventilator and the boarded-up window, darkness and isolation from the world, and more noise than I could bear. At the very sight of it, I began pushing up in my bed with what little strength I had, trying to back away from it all as I started crying out loudly, "No! Please, no!" Mercifully they did turn the ventilator off for a bit while I adjusted to it.

While Jeri's importance to me was already on the rise, the Covid isolation solidified this stuffed bear's role in my life. He was and to this day is my

Wilson (from the movie *Castaway*). I looked to Jeri for basic "human" interaction. My mind was scattered in a thousand ways. Shards and remnants were all that remained. We talked about it. We talked about how having already survived when survival was an impossibility, we now had Covid. Death had come knocking again, almost certain to undo us. We were alone, all alone. I still had trouble texting or calling on my cell phone. I was quite overcome with uncertainty about why my beloved Nancy, who had been so much by my side, was no longer visiting us (as well as others who had been so faithful to come see me, such as my friend, Jay Wright, and colleagues and friends Rev. Kendra VanHouten and Fr. Masud Ibn Syedullah).

But we understood. We understood that the strain of the long haul had overtaken Nancy. I was deeply wounded and worried that I had been simply mean to her. She had left. That was all Jeri and I could conjure up regarding this development. I hallucinated that I saw her with another man, that she was studying to become a nurse, and that she was dating a fellow student. I was, in these hallucinations, outside my room, observing them. Jeri saw what I saw, and so he understood. He understood the hurt, the pain, the anguish of losing my wife of then thirty-five years. I was devastated. I had no reason to believe that anything about my life was going to be preserved: not my marriage, my family, my friends, my home, my career, my body, my mind, and perhaps my life itself.

This was not the first time hope had died on my journey to the summit of Mount Sinai. I don't know the timeline, but I do remember the experience. I think it was shortly after my second transplant. I hadn't come to a full awareness that I had even had a second transplant operation. I only know that I felt worse than ever, and the hallucinations raged. I knew also that physically I was overcome and my spirit, experiencing the death of hope, had also given up. It seemed like my physical distress was never going to end. I wanted to end it. But I also could not communicate. I could only motion.

Every person that I encountered I tried to tell that I wanted all the life-supporting measures stopped. The tube running from my nose to my stomach, the tube in my trachea for the ventilator, the IV needle in my bruised and scarred arm, the blood pressure monitor, the pads on my chest to monitor my heart, the boots on my legs to keep blood flowing so as not to clot—all of it—I wanted it to cease. I would make a scissors motion with my fingers. Mostly people would pretend that they didn't know what I was trying to say though I later learned Nancy and Kendra had talked about it.

The irony was that I was getting better, but it certainly didn't feel that way. I just wanted to die. I wanted to be free of it all. I was thinking about dying, frustrated that I could not communicate because of the trachea tube. It meant that if I were going to die, if this torture of body, mind, and soul was to ever end, it was in my hands.

The staff wanted me up and sitting in a chair as often as possible for as long as I could. Part of the reason was to engage my core again and gain strength in general, but it was also necessary to give some relief to the many deep pressure sores that covered my back. At first, even five minutes would seem like an eternity of pain and torture. The circulation to my extremities was also of concern. Time had stood still for me. I thought I would never be released. I began to believe the nightmare that had become my life would simply go on and on and on. I believed that this would be my reality from then on and that Mount Sinai would be my home.

One day I sat in my chair slumping and thinking, thinking about how to end it all. My first thought was that I needed to make sure that my family was covered by insurance, and I needed it to look like an accident that might happen in the hospital. In my liminal fog, I couldn't remember if New York was a right-to-die state or not. I wanted to ask someone, but even if I managed to get my message across and the answer was no, then I reasoned, I would be put under watch and the path to self-annihilation blocked since they would certainly then have grounds to think I had tried to kill myself. It is a desperate thing to think about killing oneself. I even worried that if I asked, they would put me in a protective cell with protective gear on me, or restrain me, as they had to do on occasion, and this was again unimaginable to me with all that was already attached to me. Of course, none of this would have happened, but I was simply not in a frame of mind to know this.

My thought was that I could slump forward when I was in the chair and fall on my fragile head and bleed out. That would look like an accident I reasoned. I have never thought about taking my own life at any time before this. I moved closer to the edge of the chair. Finally, the suffering and pain would be over. Finally, the hallucinations would end. Finally, the suffering would cease. Finally, my mind would be at peace. I slumped forward closer, closer. I was aiming to position my head just right so that it would contact the floor with full force. Then a terrible thought flashed across my mind.

What if I fell in such a way that I didn't die but only hurt myself, broke a bone, or snapped my neck so that my condition was only worsened and not ended? What if I only managed to paralyze myself and not kill myself, making my situation worse rather than ending it? I couldn't even imagine being in the state I was in and adding to it the unthinkable prospect of being paralyzed. I slowly retracted my position. Then I sat weeping knowing that there was no escape, no relief, and certainly no hope to be had, and "not-hope" was born. I wept.

In the book of Proverbs, we find this: "Hope deferred makes the heart sick" (Prov 13:12a). Hope deferred is awful. I have frequently seen, and experienced, hope deferred. However, hope, when it is assassinated, kills and buries the soul at the same time. It extinguishes being. Hope deferred and hope dead are daemons of lesser and greater degrees. It is remarkable that when hope dies, God, too, seems to die. In the absence of hope, when it is truly gone and not just deferred, God also seems absent.

Deus Absconditus is a weighty theological term. *The Absent God.* The origins of this concept go back to the prophet Isaiah. "Truly, you are a God who hides himself" (Isa 45:15a), says the prophet. In translating this verse into Latin, the early Church Father Jerome rendered this concept into the tidy phrase "*Deus Absconditus.*" Luther, Calvin, and other Reformers used the term to form theologies around this idea. But there is the concept, and then there is the tangible encounter with the concept, the intersection when it is no longer conjecture or rumination, but real. To experience the *Deus Absconditus* is to experience the death of hope.

In the fury of the strife within me, I concluded that when hope is dead, the only thing remaining is faith. Faith is the self-willed resignation to God's sovereignty whose presence quite often is a form of *Deus Absconditus.* Faith is never a reasonable proposition. It is a revolt. It is a violent protest grounded in a firm conviction that the God who hides is also the God who is.

C.S. Lewis, in his trenchant and entertaining work *The Screwtape Letters,* presents an interaction between a demon in training and his supervisor: "Our cause is never more in danger than when a human, no longer desiring, but still intending to do our Enemy's will, looks round upon a universe from which every trace of Him seems to have vanished, and asks why he has been forsaken, and still obeys."[3] This is referred to as persistent faith. It is faith in isolation. It is the "nevertheless I believe." Faith in such isolation from its virtuous companions is wholly unreasonable. Faith,

---

3. C.S. Lewis, *The Screwtape Letters* (New York: Harper Collins, 1996), 40.

unmoored from hope, is an indefatigable persistence of belief against material odds.

This understanding is not particular to my circumstance. It is clearly seen in the narrative of Job. In the midst of suffering Job says: "If I go forward, he is not there; or backward, I cannot perceive him; on the left he hides, and I cannot behold him; I turn to the right, but I cannot see him" (Job 23:8). In the light of all that has transpired, Job's wife questions him: "Do you still persist in your integrity?" (Job 2:9a). Job remarkably states that he will keep his integrity in all his suffering and loss. For Job, it amounted to this: even if God abandons covenant, Job will maintain his side of the bargain. He will believe. His faith, and thereby his integrity, will persist in the face of the terrible *Deus Absconditus*.

The author of Hebrews links faith and hope. The translation of the famous verse usually runs along these lines: "Now faith is the assurance of things hoped for, the conviction of things not seen" (Heb 11:1). I have difficulty with that translation now. With liberties taken, I translate it: "Faith is the having-of-foresight into the essence of reality." Faith can be, as in the case of Job, a willful persistence, even when hope dies within. I believe now that faith can and often does exist even when hope does not accompany it. For this to occur, a deep plunge into reality itself must occur. Faith at its very foundation must gaze into something far beyond itself, and there it must posit belief.

When a soul arrives at this point, between the death of hope and the persistence of faith, there are tiny artifacts from a life lived and rooted in faith. One of those shards for me was a part of Chrysostom's Divine Liturgy: "A Christian ending to our life, painless, blameless, peaceful, and a good defense before the fearful judgment seat of Christ, let us ask." This prayer remained with me along with other artifacts of faith buried deep in the sediment of my soul.

For me, it was a prayer of gritty, persistent faith. It was not a hope-filled prayer, but a prayer of defiance in the face of what was. I prayed when it was unreasonable. There is a saying derived from the early Christian theologian Tertullian, "*Credo quia absurdum,*" that is, *I believe because it is absurd.* Tertullian's original was something closer to, *It is certain because it is impossible* (*certum est, quia impossibile*). This is where I pitched my tent. My body, my mind, my dignity, my life, all these things were being torn away from me, but deep at my core, at the level of my essence, I had determined amid a ghastly existence that faith would not be forfeited. It had become through the course of my life the most elemental part of my essence.

I heard theologian Miroslav Volf say at a gathering: "Prayer is a revolt against that which is." The faith at my core was in open protest, and therefore I think it was itself a prayer. Faith is a prayer lived. Hope was not preparing me for death and what might lay beyond; faith was what remained amid a crushing onslaught. In such situations, when hope has died, I think that the faith which remains is the result of the care one has taken of one's soul in life. If a soul is starved at the outset of such a thing, I have no idea how the essence of a person survives.

I have concluded that care of the soul, societally now perhaps the lowest priority for people, is in fact the most important thing a person can devote themselves to in this life. Survival in the borderland of life and death is contingent upon it, or at least it was and is in my case. Faith is one of those things that seem irrelevant to most. But as theologian Jacque Ellul would protest, it is the things perceived as irrelevant that allow the universe to exist.

Still, I do believe that faith and hope are connected in a symbiotic way. When hope is entombed, the voice of faith calls to it to "come forth." Hope was at some point resurrected in me. As Red realizes after his release from Shawshank prison, I, too, can say, "Hope is a good thing." My faith, crying from a pain-riddled, bruised, broken, and emaciated body, would live to cry out to the hope buried in my destitute heart: "Come forth." I don't remember when my sunken eyes finally saw the empty tomb where cadaverous hope lay, but that day did come. When it came, with its steps falling gently in my wounded soul, it was a sound like leaves rustling far away. I began to see a future and a life. As the wonderful, familiar passage of the prophet Jeremiah came to the despondent exiles, so it came to me: "For surely I know the plans I have for you, says the Lord, plans for your welfare and not for harm, to give you a future with hope" (Jer 29:11).

Hope is a good thing.

8

The Hospital Staff: Acts of Kindness (and Cruelty)

My religion is very simple. My religion is kindness.
—Dali Lama—

It is an imponderable thing to think that so many lives came together to save mine. My doctors, nurses, techs, and personal care nurses came from all over the world. I was alert enough at times, especially as I recovered, to get to know a little about some of them. Many had stories of how they or they and their parents had come to the United States. Some came under harrowing conditions. Some had come from other parts of the country to work at Mount Sinai. Still, others had lived in the city their entire lives. They fought and survived in the dramas of their own lives. Because they did so, they were able to help me to fight and survive. They came: Hispanic, Slavic, Israeli, Arab, Germanic, Asiatic, Oceanic, Arabic, African, Caribbean, Scandinavian, American mutts, straight, gay, transgender, Republicans, Democrats, Independents, male, female, non-binary. They all played a role.

To say I had a deep disdain for racism before my stay at Mount Sinai would be something of an understatement. Now, the world has rescued me. I have seen faces and heard stories and learned names so that if such an area of my heart had been there, it would have been eradicated. My caregivers worked tirelessly, not because I was white but because I was human. And when I turned into a shriveled, gaunt, mummified specter, they still cared for me as a human.

Some of my caregivers were Filipinos. One I remember quite poignantly though I cannot remember his name. He cared. He not only provided necessary medical attention, he ministered to my soul. I recall two instances in particular. The first came when my nurse, Frank, came in with him. I had been awake for two to three nights straight with no sleep. The goal that night was to make sure I got to sleep. Frank administered both my painkiller and a sleeping aid, while the other caregiver gently rubbed my withered feet. He had a beautiful voice, gentle, soft, melodious and comforting. He sang what I think was a lullaby in his native language. After an endless inability to sleep, staring at the ceiling, I drifted off effortlessly into a much-needed sleep. In another instance, I had a long day of conscious suffering. The day was coming to an end when the same caregiver came to check on me. He asked if I knew a particular song. I nodded and he began. The lyrics reached deep into me.

It was a song of love's perseverance. The sweetness this man brought to me on that night was remarkable. In this singular moment, I was given in this song a perspective, that the sorrow of the day could also be mixed with sweetness, and that love was what endured.

It is what the Apostle Paul reminds the church in Corinth when he says: "Love never ends. . . . For now we see in a mirror, dimly, but then we will see face to face. Now I know only in part; then I will know fully, even as I have been fully known. And now faith, hope, and love abide, these three; and the greatest of these is love" (1 Cor 13:8, 12–13).

When the "then" comes, we will see face to face. Now we understand so very little about God, God's universe, and God's people. The apostle means that first we will stand before God. But he also means, I think, that we must face each other. We so often fail to do this here and now. The refusal to do so, and the truculence and stubborn persistence with which we fail to do it, lead us as humanity into never-ending cycles: cycles of violence, abuse, misuse, and injustice which plague us as bitter vestiges of the image of God roaming the earth in our plight. At the end of it all, the titanic *then,* what will endure is love.

The particular instances of love extended to me by this person will endure. On that night, when I was encouraged in song to let the cares of the day go, that was love. I needed to let sorrow go because it hung over me and invaded me like an army. We met face to face that night, two people both

The Hospital Staff: Acts of Kindness (and Cruelty)

carrying the dignity of God's image, however shattered it was. A man struggling for life, twisted and broken, and an expat from the Philippines who had managed, worked, and struggled to make a way for himself in a foreign land. It's the sort of thing we look for each day, a remarkable moment when someone gently wipes the sorrow from our brow and points us by love to tomorrow's promise and purpose.

It is difficult to recount each act of kindness I received. Sometimes it was just a smile. Sometimes terms of endearment were used by my nurses, no matter the state of my physical form. "Hi love, how are you today?" "Hey Poppy, we're just going to adjust you a bit." I remember when I was diagnosed with Covid in April 2020. As they were whisking me to isolation, one nurse called out in a plaintive voice, "Oh, Mr. Titus!" This was an expression of care. This nurse knew my journey, that I was on the road to recovery, and now another seeming encounter with death was threatening my life. That act of love will endure. Another nurse would ask, "Did you say your morning prayers? It's important."

There was a time that one nurse told me she was going to read the Bible to me every day. This was an extraordinary sacrifice for a busy nurse, especially during Covid. At times she was assigned to other floors and came during her break. At other times she came when her shift was over. This was simply above and beyond. Another act of love that will endure. In so very many ways the personnel at Mount Sinai, beyond their professional call and obligations, demonstrated care and kindness to a weary and suffering person.

Then there was Brandon. The young man who was strong, calm, certain, constant, and reassuring. He was the one who walked with me when I was struggling even to hold myself upright. When I couldn't walk, Brandon would come with a wheelchair and get me used to sitting up again. It was Brandon who caught me when wobbly and gave me the reassurance I needed to stand because he was behind me. And it was Brandon who pushed me outside onto Fifth Avenue for my first blessed breath of fresh air in eight long months. He cared for me, and I cared for him. One day he took me to a little break room with a view over the city. For the first time, I got to know him a little. He stuck with me.

Because we are human, we live separate lives. Each of these people had families, friends, and colleagues of which I knew nothing. They each came with their unique experiences and backgrounds. Each had also their struggles. Struggles, of course, affect people, their outlook, their mood, their ability to cope, and yes, the extent to which they can extend empathy. This I understood too. I can say looking back that for the better part of my journey at Mount Sinai I was treated, not only with world-class healthcare and professionalism but also the kindnesses I have just mentioned.

But there were isolated acts of cruelty or callousness. A minor case was when something had fallen off the end of my bed. There was a caregiver at the next bed, and as he made his way out, I asked if he could get it for me. Without looking at me, he continued his forward motion, bent down, picked it up, and threw it at me. It landed square on my groin area. I had a catheter, and the pain shot threw me. That was the physical pain. Then there was the added pain of not being recognized as a person. Here we, in a very concrete sense, did not see face to face. It was a quick, fleeting moment, and I am sure he was under incredible stress from the demands of the day. I remember thinking it was cruel. Maybe not intentionally, but cruel, nevertheless.

Then there was an intentional act of cruelty I do remember. I think I had just finished dialysis and needed a new IV line inserted into my arm. I had lots of problems with IVs as my veins blew out and getting new lines going was especially difficult—for the staff as well as me. They tried to place ones that would last thirty days, but inevitably they would infiltrate and have to be replaced. Often, they required a vascular team to come with an ultrasound device to find a vein that would work. Added to that difficulty, early on both of my arms were compromised and swollen to twice their normal size. My right arm was completely bruised, a dark purple-black, and bleeding from the crease of the elbow. My left arm was weeping yellow ascites fluid right through the skin and covered in places with blisters. On this day, the needed IV was attempted over and over. One nurse couldn't do it, and each attempt was excruciatingly painful. I think she quit, I mean her job, on the spot. Maybe this was in my imagination, but the next thing was not. Another nurse upset and frustrated, brutally jabbed a needle in my arm. The pain was blinding from the stab. Another nurse saw this act and rebuked his colleague moving him aside and saying: "Hey, that wasn't necessary." I think this grew into a bigger issue of a report being made, or at least talk of one being made. It was cruel, and the cruelty of it was increased because of the intention to inflict pain.

The nurse who intervened said he was sorry that happened and gently rubbed the offended area. He said I had handled it "as a true man." I later learned more of his story. He is the son of an Iranian immigrant who

The Hospital Staff: Acts of Kindness (and Cruelty)

worked as a taxi driver in the city. His father worked at that difficult job, he said, "in order that I might have a chance to do better." In this he succeeded. In the face of cruelty, he responded in love. I can only imagine the acts of cruelty this young man has faced in his life as the descendant of an Iranian immigrant. I pray that acts of cruelty toward him will be met with more potent acts of love. Cruelty does not and can never surpass the potency of love. By its design it destroys itself and must then give way to the constructive power of love. I remember the act of cruelty of that day, but it is not the thing that endures. What endures is the act of love that in its quiet simplicity shamed cruelty, crushed it, and occupied its space.

Two further examples demonstrate the kindness directed to me at Mount Sinai. They both came in my final two weeks while I was in acute rehab therapy. Desiree was a therapist that had been with me since the beginning of my journey. She was a cheerleader. When it was apparent that I was being released soon, she brought me a large stuffed sea turtle. She is Filipino, and she told me that in the Philippines, the sea turtle is a symbol of good luck. Imagine that a hospital worker during the Covid crisis took the thought, time, and expense to do that! It's a cherished possession.

And at the end, when I left my hospital room for the final time, they lined the hallway, around twenty-five caregivers, Brandon outside to the left of the door. Some I immediately recognized; others who fought for me and cared for me I did not, their names lost in a sea of suffering, delusion, and hallucination. I'm sorry about that. I wish I could remember each one of them clearly, as they deserve to be. They applauded me. They played "Pomp and Circumstance" as I walked among them looking at them, face to face, everyone masked. There stood love enduring through everything that had happened. Even as I made my way to the exit, they were coming to say goodbye, wish me well, running from their posts to get to me before I was gone. I greeted another dozen caregivers on the way out. Even as I waited on the street for Nancy to pull the car around, they came, one knocking on the window to say good-bye.

In the eight and a half months of my sojourn at Mount Sinai, love is what dominates. Yes, there were days that I was handled roughly, brusquely, and without empathy. There were more than a few of those occasions. But in eight months of intense care, parts of it that frayed at the limits of the weary healthcare workers, it may have been unprofessional but understandable. The number of people caring for me numbered into the hundreds. You cannot always filter out all the darker impulses of humanity; that is an insurmountable obstacle. But in the larger scope, the care was unparalleled, in skill and sympathy for my plight.

When I finally sat in the car to go home, even with the Manhattan traffic humming, there was a profound silence. Quiet. No beeping, no bustle, no ventilator signal, no tubes, no needles. *Then* had finally come. But at home, something happened for which I was not prepared. I missed my caregivers. I missed the community that had surrounded me at Mount Sinai. They were like sure-footed sherpas who guided me down the summit to my release back into the world. Now, I grieved the loss of their presence. Some I have seen since then, of course. Many I will never again see, at least not on this side of the vale of tears. But I am certain that someday will come, *then*, when we see each other face to face, understand each other fully, and obtain that which endures from here into eternity itself: love.

9

The Community of Faith

The Christian Church does not exist in Heaven, but on earth and in time.

—KARL BARTH—

There was an unprecedented outpouring from our community of faith. I use the singular, but numerous bodies in our Reformed community (and beyond) became involved in my, and by extension, my family's struggle. It was overwhelming. What these communities did was, to put it precisely—Christian. Christian beyond measure. Christianity in the extreme. To use a bit of vernacular, Christianity on steroids.

The beginning of this outpouring was from the congregation that I served when this journey began, St. John's Reformed Church in Red Hook, New York. From the very point when Nancy and I announced that I would need a transplant to the hopeful prospect that this was happening to the twisted turn of fortune and events, St. John's was there. Not just in some "we'll be praying for you" vein (which I do not take lightly), but also by putting wings to the actions rooted in those prayers, in substantial and material ways.

On the side of everything going right, it meant that the consistory and congregation of the church first agreed that they would maintain my full pay and benefits through my anticipated hospital stay and recovery, expected to be about four to six months. During this time, they would also need to fund an interim minister. My short-term disability insurance covered some of this expense but not all of it, and it also meant they were agreeing to not having their full-time minister during this period. All of that is extraordinary by any measure. No one anticipated things going sideways.

Then sideways came. Each setback and each procedure set my return further and further out. At each reset of the timeline, the consistory and congregation of St. John's moved with us like clockwork. They never blinked. Financial love gifts were given. A benefit dinner was held. Then Covid hit. Mount Sinai was perhaps *the* epicenter of the first major U.S. wave of the pandemic, but the world was affected, too, and this meant churches. Finances dwindled, and resources became harder to come by. For smaller churches like St. John's, financial survival was difficult. They never blinked. They had to close; they were facing crisis upon crisis, but concerning us, they never blinked. The interim minister had to resign because of health concerns related to the pandemic. They never blinked. Had they chosen another way, my family would have been cast to the wind, and we would be in a different reality today.

When April rolled around and I was still in the Transplant Intensive Care Unit with no idea when I might even leave the hospital, Nancy and I had to talk about how my condition was affecting the church in the long term. My body and mind had been devastated and the likelihood was that I was facing at best a long recovery, if not permanent disability. By then the original six-month recovery period was fast coming to a close.

I decided to resign. Nancy, who was prevented from being at my side due to the Covid shutdown of the hospital, helped me compose a letter of resignation. (How I managed this over the phone with a trachea tube still in my neck I don't know.) But we knew that I had to let them go. Calling a Minister of Word and Sacrament in the Reformed Church in America is a long, drawn-out process that can take up to two years or more in the best of times. I needed to let them get on with that process. Also, by doing so I could focus my attention on surviving and recovering.

A minister's call is much more than a job placement. Whether shepherding a congregation as a pastor or serving as a missionary or performing another specialized ministry, a call requires more heart and spirit. As one minister colleague put it, "The call is embedded in every cell, in the core of my being." It weighs on the heart. In the case of a pastor of a congregation, a covenant is made between the minister and the church body. It took everything I had—and more—to deal with the many assaults on my physical body. I needed every personal resource I could muster just to deal with that day after day.

So, my call at St. John's needed to end. Still, they held us fast. They assured us they could wait. They didn't start any search process for some time later. In any case, the call process only became more difficult with Covid present.

I had served full-time in two congregations before St. John's as well as being an overseas missionary, but the end of this call was different. Don't get me wrong; they were all difficult, with poignancy and bittersweetness as each ministry was brought to an end. But in those endings, there was also a future and a hope, with another call to another place of service on the other side. In leaving my call in Long Beach, California, there was the promise and excitement of being a senior pastor at First Reformed Church in Fishkill, New York. In leaving Fishkill, I was going to be serving the Reformed Church in Croatia working as an advisor to the bishop there as well as serving the Evangelical Theological Seminary as Senior Lecturer in Systematic Theology. Again, the challenge and excitement were ahead. Leaving that overseas call provided the opportunity to serve St. John's.

But what of the end of this call? No, this was different. I was being taken out of the "game." There was nothing but pain, weakness, and the long work of recovering in store for me. Physical therapy, occupational therapy, speech and swallow therapy, and endless encounters with doctors. There was me and the horrible experience I wasn't yet through. And no way to know when or even how the hospital portion would end. Bitterness without the sweetness.

Mount Sinai moved the Transplant Intensive Care Unit to what was usually a surgical recovery area to provide space for the influx of critical Covid patients. That's where I was moved—to a space not designed for conscious patients. While I had lucid moments there, hallucinations were taking their toll on my mind. And then it hit. As long as my hospitalization had already been, it was going to be longer. I tested positive for Covid, just as I had started to turn a corner. My life was again under grave threat, and I was placed in isolation for six weeks. The waiting for me, my family, and St. John's became longer still.

It became longer for St. John's because even though I had resigned, they wanted to wait and see if things changed. They also were committed not only to my welfare but to the welfare of my family. They were vigorous keepers of covenant. I think many churches might have let their commitments go and cut their losses; after all, I had cut mine. They, however, looked beyond the concrete circumstance and its hopelessness. They looked into the divine. They committed themselves to the teaching of Christ. They lugged, carried, and towed themselves to the command of Christ to love, and they loved us in both spiritual and physical measure and made themselves by God's grace into a church that demonstrated the impossibility of separating those things. They were simply miraculous. That kind of thing doesn't happen overnight. A church has to be discipled that way over the years.

I loved St. John's, and I still do of course. It made resigning all the harder. I felt that I had failed them. And so, I wept at the loss. I had thought I would retire from this call, this congregation. This simply was not to be. God, in divine paradoxical providence, had other intentions. The Covid isolation and hallucinations conspired together to break me in new ways. My physical and occupational therapies were set back in considerable measure. I wasn't even allowed out of my room to walk. Whatever walking happened at that time was done in the confines of my room with a therapist in a suit better befitting a spacewalk than patient care. My recovery, it now seemed, would be interminable.

When I was released, during the height of Covid and still months before a vaccine was available, St. John's was there. Yes financially, but physically, too. When I returned home on July 10, 2020, there was the lion's share of my congregation gathered in the parking lot with masks on to greet me. I was astonished and flabbergasted. Signs and banners filled the parsonage lawn. My beloved congregation was stretching their arms out and bringing them back to themselves in substitute for the hugs we all so longed to give. Tears were running from my black, sunken eyes. Tears also came from the sky. I raised my face to let the soft rain fall upon my face, a sensation in the past I may have fled from, now just joy at feeling the water drip on and from me. The main church sign, where my sermon titles were displayed weekly, now proclaimed: "Welcome home Pastor Eric: the miracle we prayed for." I was their miracle. The one they brought into existence by living into the ideals of Christ and Christianity. My call was gone, all but officially, but I still belonged to them, a witness to something transcendent, otherworldly, and fantastic. There was something ephemeral and resplendent about it all. There I stood, all 85 pounds of me, clutching my walker as I stood in the parking lot, a light rain wetting my skin. Alive.

Alive because of and yet beyond medical agency. St. John's called me out of the tomb. They saved my family from ruin. And still, they were not finished. I was now receiving long-term disability insurance payments.

Some of the financial obligations of St. John's were lightened, but still, we were allowed to remain in the parsonage until we could get our bearings and figure out what our future would look like. They continued to pay utilities as well. This was all a remarkable gift to us. This care for us after my discharge from the hospital continued for the same amount of time as my stay in the hospital.

That I could spend eight months in the parsonage of St. John's was important also to my recovery. Going somewhere unfamiliar to me then would have been an enormous leap. I was still confused, bewildered, ever so weak, and unable to do so many mundane things I had taken for granted, like lifting a coffee mug. The mental hurdle of a new environment would have been that much more difficult. My resignation also meant that I didn't have any responsibilities at the church. That freed me to focus on my recovery. Had I still been their minister, I think I would have been back at my call far earlier than would have been wise or beneficial for my health. Because of St. John's, I was able to concentrate my energies on recovering.

Financially St. John's poured the equivalent of tens of thousands of dollars into the care of me and my family. They did so without thought of recompense. It was a free act of grace. It was love without condition. Individually and corporately, they held me up to God, praying as the widow in the gospels, persistently, with a stubbornness that wore at the eternal judge until their protest against the way things were had been met. Their cards and letters were concrete icons of that spiritual prayer, the sacrament of themselves upon God's altar, decorating the walls of my hospital rooms, when there were walls Nancy could put cards on. They filled the space and witnessed to the medical staff the love of Christ for a wounded leader. In doing all this, what had been an inevitable course toward death and ruin was transformed by this small Body of Christ, in a rural village of New York.

In the end I'm left speechless about how St. John's stepped into an unrelenting, cavernous, deadly, and dark gap for me and my family. The only words that are perhaps fitting are: "St. John's: the miracle I didn't even know to pray for."

***

Other communities of faith spanned the gap as well. The First Reformed Church in Fishkill was one of them. Fishkill is another congregation of wonderful people. I served as their minister for six years, and they were our sending church when we went to Croatia. That kept us connected during our overseas years there. The years in Fishkill were wonderful for us as a family, and Penelope, our youngest child, was born while we were there. It is a historic church, 300 years old. It served as Washington's prison during the Revolutionary War. We have cherished memories of the bustling Village of Fishkill, of kids jumping into piles of fall leaves, of winter snow stacked high next to the driveway. There are memories of cool summer evenings eating on our beautiful back deck that also housed the sandbox and the big, beautiful back yard with the beloved trampoline. It was a great place to live! I had even considered living my tenure out there and retiring from Fishkill in the still-distant future.

We deeply loved this congregation, and they loved us as well, loved us enough to recognize our call to overseas missions and champion our way there and back. The consistory and congregation of First Reformed Church supported us in this time of crisis as well. They, too, stretched out the sacrifice of prayer into God's presence on our behalf. They, too, matched this with tangible support.

Catastrophic health care and long-term hospitalization are abstract until you are living them. The main costs of treatment are covered by insurance if you are fortunate enough to have good coverage, which we did. In the Reformed Church, we have something called the covenant of care about our health insurance plan, which covers all ministers and other full-time workers across the country. We understand our profound obligation to each other's well-being.

Living through a health care crisis, especially when the hospital is in another city hours from home means extra costs mount up quickly. They can consume a middle-income budget in a blink. Travel alone becomes a wear not only on the body but also on the budget. It's not just gas, tolls, and parking costs. It is the balancing act of trying to take care of life's mundane and significant matters while fitting in a colossal exigency. It means grabbing last-minute meals from restaurants. It means picking things up while you're traveling or staying overnight. Doing laundry away from home, finding the nearest post office, even getting a short-term gym membership so Nancy could attend to her own physical needs, a myriad of concerns to be met in a secondary setting. Even with a program for housing, such as the Transplant Living Center at Mount Sinai, still there are lots of extra living costs associated with being in Manhattan for an extended time. In many real ways, the family was trying to maintain two households at the same time.

Fishkill recognized this and provided a very needed, unexpected, and extravagant financial gift to our family. I think for anyone following what was happening to me and my family, it would have been difficult not to see. We were still part of them too. Fishkill Reformed Church supported us not only when I was their minister, but also as we left them to move to Croatia. But even as we returned to the same classis (a district of churches in the Reformed Church in America) in the same county in New York to minister at a different Reformed church, we still belonged to them. Fishkill Reformed supported us with generous financial support, to say the least. This church also exemplifies what it means to be the Body of Christ. They also gave prayers, hugs, and spiritual support, a place to stay closer to the hospital at times for our children as well as a ride for one daughter at a most critical time. One family—John and Toni Houston and their girls—loved beyond words. They took our dog for months, eliminating one other issue, in a household split apart. They provided space and comfort for our children and gave a waystation of love on one particularly difficult day for Nancy, who popped in on her way back to me just to get a hug from someone who knew her.

Other congregations supported me, Nancy, and my children. Elmendorf Reformed Church in Harlem welcomed Nancy for worship while she stayed in Manhattan. They gave constant prayer and encouragement as well. One of their elders visited me often, even when I was unresponsive, and continues to reach out to me years later. Church of the Living Hope, another New York City neighborhood church, was another place of solace and peace for Nancy. Her continued virtual worship with them, after being back in Red Hook and attending the St. John's outdoor services once Covid struck its ghastly hand and closed most meeting places, helped Nancy stay anchored with me in my location during those horrible ten weeks we were separated. They prayed too. One of the ministers there encouraged Nancy with his miraculous heart transplant story and visited me in the hospital as well.

The church that I now serve, Pultneyville Reformed Church, was another that held prayer vigils for me and my family. We have a long history with them as they had opened their mission house to us for a year while we were raising support to go to Croatia and hosted us again for home assignment and when we returned Stateside. They invited Nancy to their women's retreat, which she joined in February once my condition showed enough improvement for her to be gone a couple of nights. These dear women helped to carry the emotional burden the devastation of my body was having on Nancy. They were the first to see photos of me just weeks earlier, at my worst. Other than a few ministers, my family, and a close friend, no one had been at my bedside in the long months of my stay in Manhattan. This group listened and loved on Nancy so she could come back to me refreshed from time away in the wintry calm of the Adirondacks.

The women's group of St. Christopher's Catholic Church in Red Hook knitted me a prayer shawl. I cherish it. I had come to know a few of the members of that church through ecumenical events. One I knew from the local council of churches. She and I would laugh and joke throughout these meetings and at events that brought us together outside the council. We often lamented together about the division of the church. Her name was Lillian. She was also the mother of one of the members of my consistory, or church board. Lillian was suffering from cancer at the same time I was going through my ordeal. Her priest visited me regularly at the hospital when he came to New York City to see his sister. He would pass on information about Lillian, adding that she was asking about me. Lillian passed away around Christmas time, and my heart joined the rest of my body in hurting. At her funeral mass, prayers were lifted for me, and afterward her daughter, Terry, told Nancy, that Lillian was now looking at Jesus and giving him what-for about me. A precious gift from her family to me was a prayer shawl she made, perhaps one of her last ones. Together Lillian and I suffered as part of the body, linked together in the suffering of Christ.

There were others from across the country in other places where I had served the church who also prayed regularly for me. People from my church in California were on Nancy's regular update lists and reached out with words and actions. They sent encouraging texts as they prayed. Tim and Deb Ayers, a couple we knew from years ago at our church in Oklahoma City, prayed and called Nancy—just at the moment she most needed it—when I was hours into my surgery for my second transplant. They weren't aware the second transplant was happening at that time or that Nancy was sitting in a waiting room alone, but they had felt the need to reach out and thus became the very thing Nancy most needed at the very moment she most needed it.

There were people around the world who knew and who prayed, people we loved and who loved us. Colleagues from Croatia and Romania whom we had toiled beside sent such heartfelt prayers over the internet that touched and bolstered Nancy as she tried to inform them of my condition. There were extended family members who prayed and had their churches pray as Nancy sent her regular texts. Nancy would tell everyone she was buoyed by the prayers of the people. Jacques Ellul a French theologian (and in my view a true prophet of the Church) reminds us of the Pascal formulation: "God has established prayer to communicate the dignity of causality to his creatures." Things quite often did not "go our way," and prayers seemed to fall to the ground. But God heard. There was dignity in the prayers even if immediate causal intervention did not seem to come. Prayer brings dignity to the Church in the face of suffering.

Even the World Council of Churches stepped in to provide Nancy a place to stay in a nearby hotel when she had met her time limit at the Transplant Living Center just as I had my second transplant. The Houstons jumped up to extend the time. So many in the Body of Christ came to us, to not simply alleviate our suffering, but to join in it. Even expressions carried this burden. That was the case when Nancy had to give the bad news to our Red Hook congregation that after everything I had been through and just when I was really starting to improve, I had tested positive for Covid. A small group of people had started gathering regularly for a five-minute time of simply saying hello and dropping off weekly offerings in those early Covid Sundays before the church set up the outdoor tent for services. Among that group was a nurse who was dealing with Covid's brutal sweep in her hospital. Strangely, the look of defeat and terror on her face, knowing what she knew from dealing so closely with it herself, carried the burden of our uncertainty with us and somehow bolstered Nancy.

Each of these interventions in our crisis helps me to understand better the enigmatic statement of the Apostle Paul, that he completed in his body what was lacking in Christ's suffering. Paul's statement has vexed the best of academic commentators. But the statement, far from being a slight on the passion of Christ and its completeness, means that they are in symbiotic union with each other in suffering because suffering, if we take the New Testament seriously, can be a creative and redemptive force. When Paul undergoes suffering, this suffering is "for the sake of the church." Paul's suffering is not for his sake, rather in this context, it is for the church. The corporate aspect of this is what strikes me—he suffers for the sake of the church, which itself is struggling and suffering. The apostle and his church.

The entire phrase, ἐν τῇ σαρκί μου ὑπὲρ τοῦ σώματος αὐτοῦ, ὅ ἐστιν ἡ ἐκκλησία, (*in my flesh . . . for the sake of his body, that is, the church*) (Col 1:24b) is wonderful. Paul suffered in his flesh for Christ's body. This is a paradox. But it also might provide for the possibility that suffering in the flesh becomes a creative opportunity in the body of Christ. It calls forth something; it commands and signals the need for a response. This is the synergetic mystery that many commentators wish to sidestep. I no longer have this luxury. I suffered in my flesh, and because of this, the body reacted to the suffering, and something creative, something profound arose from the body, an antiphon, a reverberation, even a redemption. In my weakness, laying on a bed, broken and useless. I wonder at times whether my deepest ministry didn't happen there, when in my weakness, I was made strong. The church moved in love and selflessness, for someone like that, someone like me.

The apostle points to this elsewhere in his writings. In his correspondence with the church in Corinth, his well-known passage says: "If one member suffers, all suffer together with it" (1 Cor 12:26a). I was the suffering member, but the body suffered with me. I can't say in my suffering that I rejoiced in much of anything, my disposition closer to Job than of Paul. But the body of Christ, in these instances, joined my suffering and joined in an antiphon with me, a lament, and a longing for things to transform. I believe we were all transformed according to God's will. In some this may have seemed minor or mundane, to others, however, such as myself, this had profound implications.

Too often I think the body of Christ, that is, the church, chooses to distance itself from suffering. Perhaps we pray about it, but entering it, that is where the transformative and creative takes form and becomes incarnational. Something tells me these communities of faith were transformed in great and small ways because they chose to enter and participate in my suffering and the struggles of my family.

There is often talk in some circles of Christianity about having a "personal relationship with Christ." The phrase now carries with it a great deal of baggage. What I can say with certainty is that I have a communal relationship with the body of Christ. This now carries for me the preponderance of what it means to be in relation with Christ, that is to be in fellowship with his body, that is, the church.

From time to time, this is a difficult relationship in which to exist. It can be ugly and hopeless. The body can look mummified at times, in the throes of death. One simply wishes to walk away from it all. But we have a communal relationship with Christ, and by way of that, each other. In my suffering, when I looked like a mummy, and undoubtedly smelled like one, the Body of Christ was for me, for us, given for us. My suffering became their suffering.

And then, one summer's day in July 2020, in the midst of global suffering, we rejoiced together, the body and me, the body and us. People gathered at two different locations. At first were a number of ministers from my classis as well as others from St. John's and beyond. I remember two of these colleagues coming to my bedside at Mount Sinai, deep in the darkest days of my plight. They sang the doxology then. They sang it again with the others that had gathered from church and village. It had a different sense to it now. The first time was to praise God for providential care, a surrender to God's care and sovereignty in the face of the enemy of death. The second was a doxology of triumphant praise. I stood in front of them as they sang in the parking lot of the Hannaford grocery store where Nancy worked. And then later, some caravaned with us to the parking lot of our church, where additional members of my congregation were waiting to greet me.

Their triumph stood before them. I was on my walker, a miracle, their miracle, the one for whom they had prayed. A miraculous ruin, a picture of the suffering which is reflected in each life of the members of the Body of Christ. I think if we are honest, we are all like this image on that day. Glorious ruins who reflect the suffering of Christ, and who in that suffering continuously sing our doxology to God, and in our prayers, we become dignified before God and the world.

10

The Sound of Silence

The most important thing for survival is communication with someone.
—Senator John McCain—

Gasping, trying to find a way to communicate, with hand outstretched, I tried to convey the most basic of things without success. This was my lot after the tracheostomy on January 9, 2020. I had taken words for granted since the moment I first began to speak. My father used to say that my middle initial *J* stood for *jabberbox*. I took sound coming from my mouth as if it would always exist. Yet, there I lay in silent astonishment that no one could hear my voice, nor comprehend what I was trying to say. It was a tragic, almost comic irony that I, a preacher and a teacher, was unable to give voice to any thought at all. Thought without the means to express that thought is more than frustrating: it is maddening! So much of our lives are dependent, day in and day out, minute to minute, on our ability to convey thought. We can get frustrated, even in ordinary conversation, when someone does not understand what we say. How much more so when speech is withheld, or linguistic hurdles are placed in our path?

I was quite unaware of why I couldn't talk. I knew that my neck had been ripped into, but the reality behind this was clouded by my mind's hallucinogenic construct of a horrible apocalyptic narrative. This I remember, although it is difficult to find words to express now, even though my ability to speak is present. Again an irony.

The Sound of Silence

Speaking has been a large part of my life. That may seem like a statement almost anyone could make. But you see, I'm a minister and teacher. This means my career is dependent upon my voice, and my ability to communicate clearly and effectively. I knew that I was going to be intubated, which means a tube is placed through the mouth down the throat into the trachea or windpipe. This tube was connected to a ventilator for the first transplant surgery. We had been informed that we should expect that I would remain on the ventilator until the following day. I had done so well through the surgery, however, that I was taken off immediately afterward. My lungs were strong, probably from years of public speaking. However, as my condition worsened in November and December, I fell into a sepsis-induced hepatic coma and again required the ventilator. After surviving that, doctors wanted to protect my lungs and so decided to do a tracheostomy, which allows the ventilator tube to be inserted directly into my airway below the throat, both more long-term and more comfortable than the tube going there through my mouth and down the back of the throat with supports on my face to keep it in place.

It's difficult if not impossible to speak if you have a tracheostomy. Speech occurs when air passes over the vocal cords at the back of the throat. Following a tracheostomy, the air that is exhaled passes through the tracheostomy tube rather than over your vocal cords. The result is no sound. I had to position a special device or my finger over the opening in my neck to close it in order to speak. I didn't always remember that I needed to do this. I do remember how futile and frustrating it was to get a caregiver's attention without the gift of speech. I would try and wave my arm or make eye contact usually to no avail.

I was so in need of speaking that I managed to form words notwithstanding my tracheostomy. Nancy tells me that some were astounded that I was able to do so. But the need to communicate, to connect with understanding, is basic. It is, as Senator McCain put it, essential to survival. I think my profession also may have played a role. I have spoken from pulpit and lectern for nearly thirty years. Your lungs and diaphragm strengthen through this process if you've been properly trained. It is perhaps a cliché, but it is often said that preachers preach to save others. I had preached, and perhaps I saved myself.

There are, of course, other means of communication beyond speech. However, even these were not at my disposal. Nancy brought me a small erasable whiteboard. I was certain that what I scribbled was clear, but even here I could not communicate. What others saw were just squiggly lines where I had hoped to convey simple needs. Nancy kept that board with my squiggles on it. Looking at it after I got home, I tried to imagine how I ever thought that those runes were legible. She said my speech even when heard was sometimes similarly garbled, though I had thought it clear.

I was brought a card in which pictures of things such as ice, heat, or pillow were depicted for me to point at. Weakened and fogged I had a hard time understanding what the pictures were trying to depict, and sometimes what I needed wasn't on the card. A frustration set in and at times I didn't even know where the card was. The ability to use my phone was beyond me as I could not use my hands to even hold my phone, let alone create a text. I had no voice. I could not write. Even conveying the simplest need was at times beyond my ability. Me a Yale graduate. Me a holder of a doctorate in theology. Me a scholar, preacher, writer, and professor. Me helpless. Me reduced to silence. Me alone, very alone.

My hallucinations grew in elaborateness and in urgency. There was danger all around, a catastrophe coming, and I could convey none of this to the people around me whom I believed needed to prepare. My actual survival and basic needs were on the one side; my journeys into other worlds created in my mind were on the other. The amount of severe stress that my hallucinations were causing was something of which my caregivers knew nothing. I was trying to live in a bed as a very ill man and have my needs met, and yet I had the responsibility, a very real responsibility in my mind, to warn them all of the dangers coming and yet I could do neither. It is a wonder that either my body or my mind or both did not simply collapse. To this day I do not understand why I am not some sort of man with incapacitated thoughts, muttering cacophonous nonsense in a corner, who looks at all of reality like a mirror into another place.

To be unable to communicate and at the same time be "out of one's mind" and struggling profoundly to survive bodily, this is an unholy triumvirate. It was the confluence of these that made my life unbearable. Every moment was full of disquietude. When I reached out trying to connect with people, I found it frustrating. They in turn also found it difficult to communicate with me.

Then the other irony. The words of the Apostle Paul: "How shall they hear without someone to proclaim him?" (Rom 10:14), without a *preacher*, come to mind as I think back to then. I tweak this just a little in my mind "How shall they hear if their preacher *can't* preach?" This was very much on my befuddled mind. I couldn't make sense of anything. How was I going to do my job? Eventually, I concluded that part of my life was over.

Frustration and futility sat with their weighty substance, and silence filled me with dread. The little things those of us who can speak don't think about. Passing by someone on the street who says "hi," and not being able to give a reply. Perhaps I would be judged to be rude. All of life's little transactions would not happen with the ease I was used to. The simple operations of life escaped me because speech was not present. Simple requests were now a production of gasping and gesticulating. Even please and thank you were taken from me. I don't remember ever giving thanks to God for being able to speak. I do recall on many occasions in my life praying that I wouldn't have to preach anymore: it is a monumental task to ask of anyone Sunday after Sunday for years on end. Now that prayer was answered, albeit in a completely different way than I ever could have imagined. Prayers are curious in that way. I've been more careful lately. Perhaps that sounds superstitious; I can live with that.

Prayers don't have to be spoken, but most often mine are. Not just public prayers that I give as a part of being a minister but also my intimate personal prayers. My cries to heaven for my family, my churches, my friends, this sore, sin-sick world—all snuffed out. The Jesus prayer I whisper throughout the day—the sound and rhythm—quenched and shushed. Yes, prayers of the heart can be done in the silence of the mind. But there is something mysterious, unable to be apprehended, and uncelebrated about the sound of prayer, something incarnational about a voiced prayer. There is a different energy about it. In this way, I would say that voiced prayer has a touch of the sacramental about it. The voice and vibration are the elements of this sacrament.

Yet, prayer can still happen. God can still understand the trials we have. The Psalmist says that God knows the secrets of the heart. Speaking to others without voice, however, is another matter entirely. There are other ways, of course, but not in the range of my ability at the time. I wondered whether this was going to be another thing I had to live with. Would I be permanently unable to speak with others? These were things I didn't know and filled me with dread as each day slowly crept by.

When I swallow now, I am still aware of the tracheostomy. I can feel that it happened. When I look in the mirror I can see the scar; it speaks to me. My scar is an ever-present reminder of the gift of speech and communication of any form. We can cry out to each other, speak words that heal, and rejoice in life. We also have the power with our speech to hurt, to scar, to even take the voice of another away. We can speak truth or falsehood. We can tease or harass. We can sob or laugh. We can also encourage, console, joke, rejoice, and cheer. Think of that. It's powerful. All of that can be gone in a moment, leaving us crying without sound. This was my fate then. Tears fell silent into my pain-haloed pillow, but there was no sound. Sound, I came to realize in those moments, days, and weeks, was such an integral part of my life, and yet, I had never given it a thought.

II

Mountain Men

Doubly happy, however, is the man to whom lofty mountain tops are within reach.

—John Muir—

A t times of lucidity, I loved to watch *Mountain Men*, *Life Below Zero*, or *Wicked Tuna*. Many times, there were marathons of the episodes. I loved the men and women in these series. I loved and longed for the life they had. I desperately wanted that life. I loved the liberty they had and the independence they worked for. I wanted it all. They hunted, caught, or grew their own food, built their own houses, enjoyed fresh air, and crisp snow under their feet. I longed to climb on the back of a horse and make my way through wandering woods. I craved the challenges they faced and the ingenious ways they met them. Mostly I yearned for freedom.

From October 29, 2019, until June 17, 2020—seven and a half months!—I had not been outdoors. On very few occasions, I had a bed with a window that I could see out of. Even in those times when I could see out, I couldn't see anything but sky and the peaks of buildings. I had not felt the wind on my face. I had not heard a bird chirp, a car running, or a dog barking (except in a hallucination). I had not seen a leaf fall, a child running, a flower bloom. There was no rain on my back, no sun on my face, no snow crunching under my boot, no water to calm my soul. The Catskills of the Hudson Valley, visible from my front porch back home, became a memory, walking to my mailbox a distant dream, the smell of flowers and freshly cut grass a faded reminiscence, the fellowship of friends lost. The turning leaves of autumn with their resplendent color had morphed into stark winter and blooming spring all without my seeing any of it.

For eight months and one week, I had not been able to get up and go to the bathroom. I envied my roommates who were allowed to get up and go by themselves. I did not have a shower or bath, only cleanings given to me by others as I lay mostly helpless. Anything that I did, I did in bed. My most intimate and basic needs, my private needs had to involve others. At 57 years of age, I had to call for assistance if these needs had to be attended to. It was demoralizing and distressing to be in such a situation. It was embarrassing and anxiety-producing. For the most part, I was treated with respect and dignity, yet I felt most undignified. I, in turn, had immense respect for the people who would take on such a job. I yearned for freedom from this daily and never-ending situation. But I also came to understand something else about dignity, something Gandhi reflected upon. We all must weather the storms of life but how we do so makes the difference. I was in a Category Five hurricane. I watched how these mountain men and women weathered the literal storms nature threw at them. I saw that the way in which they weathered them was what brought dignity to them.

As a minister, I've had the privilege of watching people weather a lot of severe storms, and I've seen all kinds of reactions to them. I've seen people navigate the most impossible circumstances with honor and nobility. But I've also seen almost complete meltdowns over the most trivial of things. Even here, though, I tend to shy away from judgment because these meltdowns over trivialities are usually (not always!) because the person is battling a much larger storm than I am privy to. The storm I was navigating was monstrous and unreal in its breadth and scope. I hope that the dignity of my humanity somehow managed, despite the storm, to have been preserved.

Some of my final weeks were spent on the transplant recovery floor. Here I was in a private room because I had had Covid. While I wasn't outside, my window overlooked the atrium of the Guggenheim Pavilion at Mount Sinai Hospital designed by the great architect I.M. Pei. I have always loved Pei's designs, but the Guggenheim Pavilion is now my favorite. I didn't have a direct view of the outside, but I had Pei's design. Sunlight flooded into the open area just outside my window. It bounced, refracted, and reflected off the windows facing the atrium. Light was starting to come into my world again. I would sit by the window looking out as I talked with

Jeri, dared even again to think at times of the possibility of a life outside of Mount Sinai.

The hours of *Mountain Men* turned my mind to the most concrete things I could do to start living that life of freedom and independence. I walked as much as I was allowed. It was difficult. Managing even one step seemed like climbing Everest. Pain swept over me, and just the act of getting on my feet to walk was a challenge. Almost invariably, I would need to call for pain medication after my walk. Still, I had larger aspirations.

I began to eat again during my last trip through the transplant recovery. The trays of food were more manageable. Yogurt was a staple. The tracheostomy in my throat had left me with a swallowing problem as material entered my windpipe instead of my esophagus. I was restricted to certain foods, and I could only drink liquids that had been thickened. Thickened water, thickened milk—quite unpleasant! I was still being fed through a feeding tube through my nose to supplement my caloric intake. Eating on my own brought the hope of having my feeding tube removed. It meant a very significant step in the journey from dependence to independence.

Independence. I wonder what that word means. I was so dependent for the longest time. Independence. I get the concept. I am, after all, an American. I grew up learning the importance of the Declaration of Independence. I was taught we are an independent nation made up of people who value, perhaps above all else, independence. It is so tied to our understanding of freedom. The Declaration of Independence was a shaking off the tyranny of the English monarch. "We don't need your help. We don't need your interference," we proclaimed. But even independence here was not without the caveat of America's national motto, *E pluribus unum*, out of many one. That speaks of the necessity of *interdependence*. It was clear that the various territories of the colonies, if they were to be independent of Great Britain, had to be dependent upon one another to survive. Even within national understanding, then, independence is a myth, an illusion we entertain at the expense of truth. *Self-sufficient* might be a better word. My Christian understanding is different than this. Honestly, if I take Christian Scripture with any seriousness at all, it flies in the face of the idea of independence as we typically understand it. We draw distinctions in so many ways. The terms *assisted-living* and *independent-living* facilities are examples of this. *Freedom*, I think, is a better term and what I longed for. I wanted to be free. Christian canon points to a different sort of freedom, real freedom.

I struggled to be free. I hallucinated about being free. Early in my stay, I believed a rescue operation was being launched to get me out of Mount Sinai. I asked my wife in my delusions to have our son Samuel bring me a grappling hook and rope because I needed them for the escape. I even thought that my critical care nurse was in on the great escape. A helicopter and SUV had been procured by my friends to help facilitate my retrieval. Painfully humorous then to those that heard me talking such nonsense as if we had cat-burglar gear waiting in our garage, but painful to me then and painful still. My mind was expressing in its constructs, the force and desire of my will to be free, free of it all—the pain, the suffering, the confinement, the tests, the needles, the incisions, the horror of it all.

What we Christians see in Scripture is a different view of freedom. Instead of the notion of doing what we want to do when we want to do it, something different emerges. In the gospel of John, Jesus says: "And you will know the truth, and the truth will make you free" (John 8:32). How does one know this truth that makes one free? Jesus says it is through understanding his teachings. Many Christians in America today are woefully alienated from Scripture. That is the fact of the matter. Even in the off chance that they know what the words are, they are lacking in understanding them, and even more egregiously, are found wanting when living them. This, of course, means that far from being free and independent, they are imprisoned as they walk through life. To be bound (dependent!) to Christ means to be obligated to his teaching to be free.

The Apostle Paul says in his first letter to the church at Corinth, "Or do you not know . . . that you are not your own? For you were bought with a price" (6:19b, 20a.) I am not my own. I can't do whatever I want to do, whenever and however I deem. The American notion of ultimate personal freedom is antithetical to Christian life. To "live free or die," in a Christian context, means that we will follow the teachings of Christ or die trying. We are commanded by Jesus to love our neighbor as well as our enemies, or we die trying. We love God with all our heart, soul, mind, and strength, or we die trying. That we are not our own also flies in the face of American values. We have an overhyped notion of "inalienable" rights. This may be true for us as American citizens, but it is not true for us as Christians. Because we are bought with a price, all "our rights" are immediately and without question "alienable."

There is no doubt we all long to be free and independent (in the ordinary, daily, usage of the word). As Christians in America, we walk "freely and independently," but we do so under God's reign and rule. We may struggle at times with this. We may wish to "be sprung." We may even be in dire straits, but Christians are only "free indeed" when they have heard, understood, and performed the teachings of Jesus Christ, full stop.

The Apostle Paul states in his second letter to his protege Timothy, that he is bound in chains but that the gospel is free. Paul was free even though imprisoned. He was free because he was bound to the gospel. His captors, though, while seemingly free, were bound—because they were not so bound to the gospel. Truth evaded them; therefore, freedom also evaded them.

I was bound. Bound to tubes and needles. Bound to a bed. At times I was physically restrained because in my state of confusion and hallucinations, I would pull out the things that were projecting from my body—feeding tube, IVs, drainage tubes. I even tore at my tracheostomy tube. I would wonder why I was immobile. I would hallucinate all sorts of terrible and impossible reasons for the way things were. I would construct worlds to explain it, to see if I could get to the root of being bound. I desperately clung to the dream of being independent and free, but freedom from the tyranny of my plight was elusive, my sentence interminable.

The root of being bound is every attempt to subvert the gospel of Christ and free ourselves from it. The root of freedom, for every Christian, is to follow in word and deed, the teachings of Jesus. Sure, I wanted to be a mountain man; however, I was Job. But Job was a free man despite all his suffering and loss.

At some point, early on in my odyssey, I had determined something concerning my faith. Job was prompted by his less-than-encouraging wife to, "Curse God, and die." Job's response tells of his character and integrity amid suffering and loss: "Shall we receive the good at the hand of God, and not receive the bad?" It is then noted that "in all this, Job did not sin with his lips" (2:9, 10). In short, he was determined in the middle of all his various disasters to bless and not curse God. I was Job. I determined that I would not curse God. I didn't. Something inside told me this was important. I heard other voices too: "Curse God and die." If I did, I felt like I would be chained to negative things: anger, bitterness, hate, isolation from God, in violation of my covenant promises to God. Would I receive the good but not the bad? No, bound as I was, I was bound more intricately and intimately to Christ, who stands against such things. To curse God was to curse myself, who I am at my core.

When we are bound to suffering, even to the point of fighting the enemy of death, I think something else emerges. The Apostle Paul, in praying for his infirmity to be taken from him is told that God's grace is sufficient and that in human weakness, God's strength is revealed (2 Cor 12:7b–9). Looking back, I can't say that I knew at the time that God's grace was sufficient, but I do think that God's strength reveals itself. Sitting in the transplant recovery unit in my final weeks, feeling mostly in my right mind, I was able to reflect because I knew I was recovering. I was up on a walker. I could make slow laps around the unit. I could sit in a wheelchair in an observation room looking over part of Manhattan, speaking gently with my physical therapist. I felt something I hadn't felt in a long time, the presence of God. Jeri and I listened to daily Scripture readings from the Revised Common Lectionary. On more than one occasion, I was asked by my nurse if I had said my morning prayers! I was stunned, finally, to know health care providers understood that my soul was also struggling to survive. Those readings and my times of prayer were different then. They had a strength and power to them.

Those readings plunged deep into my soul, and I often wept when I heard them, as they came so close to how I felt and what I had endured. In all of my shatteredness, in my utter feebleness, God was strong, and I felt that strength. I am reminded of the Apostle Peter who wrote: "Now for a little while you have had to suffer various trials, so that the genuineness of your faith—being more precious than gold that, though perishable, is tested by fire—may be found to result in praise and glory and honor when Jesus Christ is revealed" (1 Pet 1:6b–7). I have suffered many trials in my life, but nothing of this magnitude.

Fire is used elsewhere in Scripture as a metaphor for purification. In the Torah, the book of Numbers states about real, substantial objects: "Everything that can withstand fire, shall be passed through fire" (31:23a). This was to make sure the object was clean according to the law. I was put through the fire. Amazingly when I came out, I felt clean in my soul. In this early time, both at Mount Sinai and at home, I felt spiritually pure, very much like a child unencumbered with the filth of life. Dostoevsky sums it up this way: "A healthy man is always an earthly, material man . . . when he falls ill, and the normal earthly order of his organism is disturbed, then the possibility of another world makes itself known to him at once; and as the illness worsens, his relations with this other world become ever closer."[4]

---

4. Jean-Claude Larchet, *Theology of Illness* (Crestwood: Saint Vladimir's Seminary, 2002), 60.

Often, I think back to that image of Jeri and me sitting by the window. It's more than a thought; it is more like I am an observer of a moment locked in time. It is like I am standing in the room looking back at me then. As odd as it sounds, because I was still in a time when "relations with the other world become ever closer," I find myself wanting to be there again, in that moment, broken as I was. I was other-worldly. I'm not sure how to recapture that now. Maybe it is something that I stumbled into that only mystics and saints know how to touch with regularity.

I suppose, upon reflection, I can say this, I was a mountain man. I climbed to the summit of Mount Sinai, and I saw and touched the fire that only a sovereign and providential God can generate. I felt the awful grace of God. I saw the burning bush of Moses. I touched it, and I was clean. I was God's mountain man.

12

Crossroads

Jacob was left alone; and a man wrestled with him until daybreak.
—The Book of Genesis—

Snow is falling today. I watch through the window as it slowly descends. I see how freely, and how innocently the flakes tumble. I commune with Jeri, and I think of the encounter at Jabbok ford between God and Jacob. At the end of the struggle, Jacob's hip was displaced. But more than that, he changed Jacob's name and identity. Jacob was broken with a purpose. I'm not sure I was broken with a purpose, but there is a brokenness that remains and a new identity emerging from my struggle. I have a sense that in my long wrestling match, I too, in my own way, encountered God at Mount Sinai. The story of Jacob expresses how I feel most of the time since coming home: broken. I search for who I am. There is a melancholy in my soul today. It is a soft and sad melancholy, comforting in some ways, like the sight of the snow. I catch a glimpse of my wrist and see a scar, and I remember my struggle and my encounter.

There is not much of my body that is not scarred. Either scarred by major surgeries, drainage tube insertions, IVs, or dialysis tubes inserted in my neck. Needles came several times a day. Blood draws continually. Finger pricks for sugar levels. Shots to keep my blood from clotting. I have calculated that my body was cut, stuck, or punctured over two thousand times in eight months. Certainly, I was unconscious for some of those, but

I also remember being unable to control screaming or crying at others, the anguish overtaking me.

I think back to December 2019. Snow was falling then too. It was one of the rare times I had a window in the hospital, until the very end of my stay the following summer. I had a feeding tube in at that point, unable to consume food without vomiting. I was also suffering from encephalopathy, a disease in the brain caused by toxicity, in my case from liver failure.

December 2019 was a crossroads in many ways. My first liver transplant from my living donor, Jackie, was failing. The altered state of consciousness set in from the surgery, the pain medications, and the encephalopathy. Delusions came. Paranoia was present. Hallucinations, terrible, indescribable, and Himalayan, set in. My body deteriorated, my mind shattered, and my spirit lost hope. Faith endured. Very little could be done for me, outside of maintenance. I felt people drifting away from me though I have been assured they were there just the same. Then came the shudder of loneliness, the sense that everything had gone wrong, and now the prospect of death was so very close and so very real. At times I even welcomed it just to be rid of the routine of cruciation. My kidneys already had failed and now the partial liver along with them. The crossroad between life and death began. But that wasn't the only crossroad that I encountered.

In the aftermath, I look remarkably the same. Sometimes I sound and feel like the old me. It is often said that everyone changes over time. I hold this to be a truism. However, in the routine course of life, we usually have some sense of familiarity with ourselves, who we are at our core, some level of self-understanding, a continuity to it all. I seem to have lost that continuity. I grieve the loss of me.

I woke from my ordeal feeling different. I experience myself as a different person, a stranger to myself. It's not like I don't like this stranger, but sometimes I struggle to remember who I was. I look at Nancy and I ask in so many ways "Do you remember who I was?" There is an emotional turmoil about it. I know and have been told that I look great and sound great. Part of that is due to the depths I came back from. The contrast now is great. In another way, I know that I look the same and at times present like I used to, but it is not as simple as that. I don't mind the observations or comments at all, but for me, there is a dissonance in it. Because of the neuropathy that courses through me, even my body does not feel like my body. My hands do not feel like my hands. My feet are not my own. But it is in the makeup of my soul that this is most apparent to me. I'm a minister trained to treat the soul. As I watched a huge medical complex and highly trained medical people attend to my body, I could not help but think how much effort and money went into the treatment of a vessel that contained my soul and how little was committed to the treatment of the essence of who I am—my soul. Yet, the essence of who I am was also at stake.

Each day I search for who I was and who I am now. There is the old me. It is buried somewhere deep inside, or perhaps it has taken flight. The old me was the me that was decisive, knew the answer, recognized exactly how to respond to a crisis, was self-assured, emotionally in control, and logical. I could do a dozen things at once, all with confidence.

Now I must admit that most of that is gone. I must face a new truth about myself. I most assuredly am at a crossroads because while I survived, I also did not survive. Part of me died. More often than I care to admit, more often than anyone would know, I'm scared. I feel small and diminished. I feel like a child at times. My physical strength and capacity have been ravaged, my identity altered.

While things are better than when I first arrived home, I realize that I am not even in the same place I was in my family. I grapple with the realization that my family functions differently. I suppose after eight months of absence this is understandable. It's hard to realize that life moved on for my family. It wasn't as though they'd forgotten me, and I know that much of their lives were impacted and shaped by my circumstances. Still, I wasn't there among them. I'm used to responding to trauma. I'm used to steering the ship. But I was no longer in the wheelhouse, and in a very real sense, I was the eye of the storm. Instead of responding to the trauma, I was the trauma. I think our family dynamic was that my wife, Nancy, was the engine, and I was the navigator. But when I left my post, I thought I would return the same, even better. It was not to be. The family coped. They continued, and the ship righted itself. My role vanished.

Eventually, in life, this happens to all of us. But people don't usually return from the dead. Where do I fit in? Especially now that I'm physically able to move without a walker and to tend to my own needs, I no longer even have the role that I first filled when I came home, that of convalescent. There is here, too, a sad realization that I am not the same person. Sometimes I feel like I am looked at differently. I'm not the same dad one could come to with trouble or need. I am that man who went through a horrible experience. I am Lazarus. I am a damaged miracle.

I hear the wind chimes on our front porch. I didn't care for wind chimes before. Now I like them. It's a tuned chime. It voices a part of Holst's Pluto. Holst designated the Pluto movement of his orchestral suite as "The Renewer." I listen and I hope. I remember that the prophet Daniel was promised that the ruined Jerusalem would be rebuilt, but that it would be done in times of trouble. I hold onto this as if it were meant for me. I believe that what I was is the seed for what I am becoming. There is at the center of my religious tradition—my faith—belief in resurrection, the promise of renewal. Perhaps I too, will be rebuilt upon the ruins.

13

Recovery and Recovering

For the human soul is virtually indestructible, and its ability to rise from the ashes remains as long as the body draws breath.

—Alice Miller—

When I arrived home after my odyssey, the first parts of the long-term recovery began. Nurses and physical therapists came to the parsonage. Maneuvering my walker through the house was difficult, and getting into the bathroom was a struggle. Putting much more load on the walker than Jeri was a real workout. Nancy had to change my coffee mug for a lighter teacup because the mug was literally too heavy for me to lift. I was so frail. I weighed about half what I had before, a mere 85 pounds. I knew that recovery, in any true, full sense of regaining myself was going to be long, painful, and perhaps impossible. The things that I had hoped for on my way to Mount Sinai that October day in 2019 were gone. In their place was me, hardly more than a skeleton, a shell-shocked mind, a soul plagued by specters of hallucinations, near-death experiences, and delusions. It was not just that my body had to be rebuilt, but that somehow my mind and my soul needed this as well.

Hobbling along on my walker I would freeze, staring not at the thing in front of me but a projected memory haunting me from my days and nights at Mount Sinai, fear and dread piled up into a singular memory of misery, still somehow mesmerizing and fantastic. Night terrors plagued me, waking me up yelling, kicking, thinking I hadn't been released at all. I had, after all, committed to the idea that I would never be released and that I would live the rest of my days at Mount Sinai. Yes, I believed I would be tied to an endless stream of physical and occupational therapy but never independent again. Eventually, my family would grow tired of visiting, needing to live their own lives, and rightly so. Reality was a proposition that was not to be trusted. Surely one of these terrible nights, I would wake up to find myself in the hospital again. Certainly, I would awaken to one of those persistent hallucinations. Truly that phase of it wasn't really over, was it?

And what of my mind? What of my highly trained and specialized mind that I had worked on my whole life? Had I not loved the Lord with all my mind? Had I not used it properly? What had all that education been about? Tens of thousands of dollars and thousands of hours robbed from my family. I had not only been a fool, not God's fool, but a damned fool. And now that was gone, too. I couldn't concentrate. I couldn't read, a true love to which I ran for refuge my entire life! How to repair all this?

One thing emerged from the fray better than the others. In utter brokenness in these other arenas, my spirit seems to have come out in better shape than when I went in. Was this the price for that? Perhaps, but a cruel God must arise out of that proposition. A God who I frankly do not understand and who escapes my mental grasp came into view. I suppose that is why the prophets spoke in such transcendent language, why Moses could not look God in the face at his Mount Sinai, and why in Christian theology God must ultimately don a human face for us to look at the divine visage at all. I think that to look God in the face, with the incarnation stripped away, is to see a God eerie and awesome (a word that in Christian parlance has lost its force). It is to see a God in singularity and plurality. It is to face a love immense and incomprehensible, without bias, without prejudice, without pride, ancient and eternal. Such a love is *unheimlich* as the Germans would say, *uncanny, spooky, surreal*. To be swept as we are into such a being would be to drown in an ocean that we cannot tread. I am still confused about why I survived at all. But somehow, I have a sense that love was involved. The love God channeled through others and ultimately the love that God is in divine being. It is still particular, odd, cruel, and inexplicable why my young donor died, and I lived. This is part of my recovery too, the grief that sits in my soul over the death of my donor.

Recovery in my body, which is still and probably always will be recovering, began in those early days at home with the physical therapist. When the home care ended, I began going to physical and occupational therapy away from home. I was committed to my body's recovery. I worked hard every painful moment of it to get better, to free myself of my walker. To be independent. Eventually, I was well enough to drive myself to therapy. I would load up the walker and be on my way. When the professional physical therapy was ending, I began at home with a more aggressive approach. Strength training with weights, planks, stretches, running (very slowly, a plod really) up a hill beside our house were all a part of my self-created program. I had moved in a few months from barely making it halfway to our mailbox at the bottom of a hill with the help of my walker to mastering that hill on my own. I drank copious amounts of protein drink. I made huge breakfasts with Jeri at my side. Three-egg omelets, bacon, sausage, toast, juice, and coffee—from a regulation mug.

Other ways I needed to recover included addressing my hearing problems, an unexpected complication from heavy antibiotic use after my second transplant. I had to get hearing aids. My eyesight also was affected. I needed a new prescription there, too. As quickly as I had lost many doctors, I was gaining new ones. I suffered and still suffer from painful neuropathy (critical illness neuropathy is the medical designation for what I have), so the pain must be managed daily. Painful joints now attend me, too.

My teeth had not been cared for normally during those eight months, mostly just getting swabbings from a nurse. I was just starting to relearn how to use a toothbrush in March 2020 when a powerful setback sent me back to the Transplant Intensive Care Unit and back on a ventilator. I remember the first time I stood with my walker in front of a mirror to brush my teeth. That was in acute rehab in July. I was absolutely shocked by my face. I didn't recognize it as mine. I slowly brushed, stunned and in disbelief.

As much as I didn't remember my face, neither did I, nor do I to this day, remember my mind as it was before. I wondered, and still wonder, if permanent damage wasn't done due to the long odyssey. The health of the body plays a massive role in the "state of the mind." Of course, the brain itself is a physical organ. Toxins not cleared by my diseased liver built up in my brain causing encephalopathy. That plus the pain meds plus the deep trauma in my body all played a role in my delusions and hallucinations.

As much as one must exercise the body in recovery, so too the mind must be exercised. Slowly things came back. Nancy brought me easy-to-read stories. Samuel played chess with me. And I studied chess; it was the best exercise for me. Not easy! Perhaps I should have begun with Candy

Land! However, here too, improvement began. Still, understanding sometimes eludes me.

The health of the mind doesn't just entail thinking but also feeling. Here is where I am most vulnerable. Harshness between people hurts. When it is directed at me, it is unbearable. I'm able to hold my ground, not break, hold my countenance, but it hurts. When I hear it coming from myself, even internally inside myself, it also hurts. I manage, barely, and a lot of energy is spent just "presenting" myself. It can be an exhausting proposition. Generally, we think about recovering from emotional damage through the practice of counseling. I've spent hundreds of hours in counseling, mainly trying to figure out how to cope with a newer, more vulnerable model of myself, as well as figuring out what happened to me at Mount Sinai. While it does have its place, therapy also has its limitations. It can't fix things with the scientific accuracy available to other healing disciplines, and if not applied by an astute practitioner, it can cause more harm than good.

Orthodox Christians believe that tears are a gift of God, a *charisma*. I have always held that to be true. Tears can bring healing. Tears are present at times of sorrow, loss, pain, distress, crisis, and even anger. They are also present in laughter and joy. They come during the recollection of memories. They come, too, in repentance. They are both a pressure valve and a balm. More than anything else, and the reason I think the Orthodox hold them as a divine gift, is that they are a symbol, expressing something of the holy and of the divine sacredness of each human. It is an irony that many people "hold them in."

Of all the tools of healing that accompanied my recovery, tears were perhaps the most effective. Tears provided the ability to physically express grief, loss, pain, anger, memory, and all the rest—because they were all there in abundance. I didn't cry that often before all this unleashed itself in my life. I guess it was because I was a child of that generation that spoke frequently about real men not crying. I think that ridiculous proposition exists in many cultures. It is viewed as a weakness. However, the Evangelist John in his gospel uses one word that expresses the power of tears: Jesus wept (εδακρυσεν—John 11:35). Its grammatical form is known as the aorist tense. In this construction, it indicates that Jesus didn't just sob a little bit to himself. He burst into tears. Everyone could see. In Christian theology, in our basic confession, the Nicene Creed, we hold that Jesus was fully human. I think John, who is more "dogmatic" about God becoming human than perhaps any other of the New Testament authors, places this in his gospel because tears cover the entire gamut of human emotion. They are not just present with grief or sorrow but also joy and happiness. This means that tears present at the birth of a person are also present when that person dies.

Recovering has brought its share of tears. They have been there in the shadow of night terror and in a new sunrise. They have accompanied me when I continually fail at some goal I am working for or the setbacks I have suffered. I also have wept when I finally found something I could do that I wasn't able to do before. They are there when I get hurt. Sometimes a day is filled with tears from dawn till dusk because I'm just in a horrible way. Sometimes a day is filled with them because I'm alive, and I now look at the fractal pattern a tree makes upon the sky as I look upward through its branches, and I think how marvelous it is. Perhaps I'm weak from all the tears, but then again, I'm in good company, I think. Tears are gifts because they heal our broken selves and our broken world. Tears help us to re-member ourselves.

When I began my recovery proper, I foolishly thought I might be able to say one day: I have recovered. I know better now. I can only say I'm recovering. I'll never recover, and just acknowledging that is a point of healing. I know that until I pass from this life, I will only always be recovering. I'm okay with that. It means that I begin to know my limitations and that some dreams that I once had will always be just that, dreams.

14

How am I Doing Today?

As followers of Jesus we can also allow our wounds to bring healing to others.
—Henri Nouwen—

Most days begin the same way for me now. I get up, have my coffee and breakfast, and watch *Morning Joe* with Jeri and sometimes Nancy. I shave, dress, and put in my hearing aids. Usually, the neuropathy starts pulsating; the pain in my back starts reminding me of the eight months spent in a bed and the deep wounds that resulted. I think about Nancy, my children, and my situation in life. I wonder if I will make it through the day without blowing apart. I hope reality doesn't start splitting apart like the Red Sea under the staff of Moses. Some days I will drag myself out of bed, knowing that my body would rather stay put. My anxiety can't face the hours ahead, and my depression and Post Traumatic Stress Disorder, PTSD, tell me it's better under the covers. At night I return to those same covers telling Jeri that we made it through another day. But my days now also hold purpose.

I have a family to love. I have a flock to tend, a people to pastor. Like a shepherd that has survived the vicious attack of a wolf pack, I move forward to guard the gate again. I do so now with a sense of the eternal about me that I've never had before. It is an undaunted sort of strength that comes from beyond me. I used to be anxious about so much, but there is a feeling of calm about ministry now and casting away of those things. I think I used to punch an imaginary corporate time clock in my head that urgently pressed me to put in my fifty to sixty hours a week. Many of my colleagues do this too. Now I only cater to the clock of my calling.

It's hard to focus at times. I don't know what to do or which way to go or what task to tackle. Sundays. Sundays are that day when I must get up, engage with the Word of God, proclaim the Good News, believe the Gospel, and confess my faith with the congregation. I meet them face to face, each with the cares of his or her own life.

Sundays especially can be troublesome because honestly the Good News sometimes doesn't come so easily to me. Because of hallucinations, the concept of resurrection is affirmed inside me, yet it also terrifies me. In some ways, I guess it should. It's an otherworldly concept, a reality springing from the font of a Godhead I can scarcely understand. It taunts my reason. It mocks me. On some Sundays, everything is well. On others, I dread the thought of simply making it through ninety minutes. Time is its own daemon.

Time can still drag for me like those long horrific days in the hospital. It reminds me of then, and how I never want to experience anything like that again. I walk each step and experience each moment knowing that my time on earth is very limited. I spend many days alone. My days with children living at home are over. Nancy, between managing our rental property, working at the pharmacy, freelance writing, and managing all our domestic affairs, is often away for hours at a time, and I feel lonely like never before. Loneliness and time are a formidable pair. It's not that I don't like time by myself. I do. In the past, I longed for it, but it was elusive. I longed for time to study, to write, to work in my wood shop, to indulge in my love for magic. Now I cannot concentrate because the vehement and strident silence distracts me. Often, I simply need the knowledge that someone from my family is in the house while I work in my study.

Memories persist and can overtake me like a thunderclap. I can freeze for a moment, remembering, terrified. I pace in circles at times. Night terrors bedevil my sleep. Nancy has to wake me to let me know I'm okay. I'm not, but her steady calming touch and her soft soothing voice reassure me. I have a depth of love for her now that was born out of time. I wish this love, the love I carry now, could echo backward to erase and heal the callousness and unconsidered zeal of youth, which leaves its tracks and injures all of us that bear the name human. I live my life in gratitude for her. I remember each day to hold her, to say to her: "Good morning, Love. I love you."

How am I Doing Today?

My physical body is often a reflection of my emotional state. It shakes or trembles. I can misstep and not know where to guide my foot. I lack energy and ambition. People have often said that I am a miracle. This I think is quite true. I am quick to say, "yes, but I am a damaged miracle." I think all miracles are. I didn't come out unscathed in any aspect of my being. My perception of things, of physical objects, is different. I have a hard time sometimes processing things when I perceive they are out of place or somehow don't belong.

Lazarus. I think about him, without fail, daily. In the account of the Evangelist John, we find the only account in the gospels of this man being brought back from the dead. It's a prolonged account. It consumes all of chapter 11 of John's gospel and concludes in the middle of chapter 12. It is substantive reading if you look at it carefully. It includes, among so much else, one of the most overt accounts of Jesus' humanity: he wept. Jesus suffered at the loss of a friend, and more than that, he suffered at the death of one of his creations. Then there is the intrigue. There is a growing conspiracy to kill both Jesus and Lazarus. Kill the miracle. Kill the story. Discredit Jesus. Problem solved.

These things are captivating. But it is what is not said that teases me and vies for my attention. If Jesus has this power, and if the death of his creation hurts him, why doesn't he just heal it? Why just Lazarus and not, well, everyone? The second of the things is, what happens to Lazarus after this? Lazarus is one of those people God chooses to point toward something greater, something future, something more far-reaching than what Jesus did on that day. As Jesus puts it, "It is for God's glory so that the Son of God might be glorified through it" (11:4). It doesn't answer the full question, but it does point to something. It's like being on the very front part of a storm, you see a drop here and a drop there. In East Texas, where Nancy's parents lived, you could see the thunderhead from miles away, and you knew something big was coming. Lazarus was a sign that something big was coming. His existence on earth was a witness to that. Like a drop of rain on a weary Texas prairie. A promise, a sign, a piece of a syndrome.

After this story, we don't know or hear anything about Lazarus. We don't even know if the assassination plot against him succeeded. But, if he went on to live a full life, what was it like? I wonder if he was changed in some way. Did he suffer from PTSD? Did other health issues dog him? Did he become famous or fade into the shadows? How did he feel about all this? He had already suffered and died, but he was going to have to die again. What did he think of that? I can imagine that he never really escaped the experience. It became what defined him. It defined him as much as his name did—Lazarus. In Hebrew it is *Eleazar*, meaning *God has helped*. Jesus, in raising Lazarus from the dead, was pointing toward something. Something colossal.

Jesus in his suffering, in his death, in his resurrection, achieved that colossal thing. Lazarus was a temporary marker; he was brought back in mortal form. Jesus was resurrected; that is a permanent stamp. It is a divine inscription, writ large upon all humanity. "God has helped." And because God has helped, God will be glorified. Herein lies the mystery. Maybe in our suffering, we are all markers. Perhaps it is as Nicholas Wolterstorff says, that we are images of God in our suffering, too, because God has suffered. Many things are now just a muddled mystery for me that I cannot solve.

I've lost count at this stage of my career of the number of funerals I have conducted. Some were poignant, others as cold as an arctic tundra. Some services filled a sanctuary. While others stood lonely and stark like Father McKenzie staring at a headstone. At the beginning of the Reformed worship liturgy for funerals these words, which I have uttered on countless occasions to an untold number of people, now stand out to me more than any other: "Let us acknowledge our grief and be open in our love, *affirming the meaning and mystery of life*." It's this last statement that now seizes my attention more than any other in the liturgy. The wonderful, damnable mystery of it all. Forty years in serious theological inquiry, and I still cannot get a solid grasp of it.

It is reputed that when the great theologian Thomas Aquinas passed away on December 6, 1273, his last words were, "Such secrets have been revealed to me that all I have written now appears as so much straw." Other accounts say that Aquinas more directly referred to the Apostle Paul's words about earthly works, that works not built on the firm foundation, would be consumed by fire—the wood, hay, and stubble. I suppose this God who resides in mystery does that to our contemplations of the divine, reduces them to wood, hay, and stubble.

I feel that way most days. In the midst of everything, I feel like I might have encountered what Moses encountered in the cleft of the rock, like I had a glimpse of something I should not have seen—Someone—antediluvian. I have become ancient. Such secrets have been revealed to me that all I have written and done now appears as so much wood, hay, and stubble. Everything that can pass through the fire, must be put to the fire.

How am I Doing Today?

Day to day there is also a quiet sadness that accompanies me. Sadness for what I lost in all this. The time I lost. The career that met the bourn. The loss of sensation, confidence, hearing, function, security, assurance, focus, who I was, and so many other things. So many ashes that my Valerie could draw a giant mural. I remember dear friends and colleagues I so admired who passed away both during and in the wake of my hospitalization. I think of the millions that died from Covid, many of them colleagues and friends. Grief is with me. I think of the young man who died and became my donor. To this day I don't know why I lived, and he died. I have even lost the ability to not show my tears. My heart is cut and is a persistent wound that will not heal. I suppose I am now what Henri Nouwen referred to as "the wounded healer." I hope that I can do that, help heal others of their persistent wounds of the heart. At least I can say that I understand, knowing there is something substantial in those words.

There are also joys I take in daily. Waking up and seeing my wife asleep by me. Holding Jeri there, too, is a joy. In each visit of my children, I give thanks for the time together. I make it a point to hug them in their coming in and their going out. I give thanks for each text that comes across my phone from them. My children are gifts to me; they are manna that never grows old. When I hear them talking and laughing together, that is a balm to a damaged soul and a wounded heart, and for the briefest of moments the impossible happens—I forget.

I can communicate. I'm able to write although my atrophied fingers sometimes fly uncontrollably, errant, over the keyboard. Nancy and I walk out to Lake Ontario and sit and watch the waves. I see again the blue sky and clouds that brighten and bedeck the heavens. There was a time I thought I would never see them again so elusive were they in those eight and a half months. Trees stand before me glorious and fractal against the sky. I try to listen as their soft message comes on the gentle, winter winds off Ontario. The lake, the other side of which I cannot see, is a reminder of how we try to describe God. It's like me speculating about what the other side of Ontario looks like although I have never seen it. Perhaps a lot like my side of the lake, but I simply do not know precisely. The lake itself looks endless. We look into a fragmented glass which is dark, as the Apostle Paul so rightly points out. I wait for the soft song of birds like I heard on that June day in 2020 when I was rolled out to the sidewalk on Fifth Avenue at Central Park for a brief time.

For now, I have a family that I love and that loves me. I have a congregation to serve that allows me to minister through weakness. I have a God, awe-ful in might, terrible, swift, the Ancient of Days, immortal, almighty, but who also exists in ineffable paradox. Love itself, the grace in which everything is grounded, the redeemer who loses nothing of creation in the end, and who pines for the children created in the image of the Divine.

There is a dread in me. The dread of returning to the borderland. I cannot forever vanquish the inevitable. Maybe I will again see that mysterious woman, who alone knew the delicate recipe that could make a linen bright and fresh like none other. Perhaps I'll see that warm, pale, green lantern light in the distance on a footpath where I stand, inviting me to cross out of the borderland into something extraordinary. Maybe then I will be healed.

Epilogue

He is your friend who pushes you nearer to God

—Abraham Kuyper—

Jeri sits a lonely vigil upon our bed. Joining him are friends: Reeses, a small bear Nancy gave me on Valentine's Day 2020 that was attached to a heart-shaped box of the peanut butter candy that would wait months before I could eat it, and Tiny Chef, a TikTok wonder who went on to get his cooking show on Nickelodeon. It never felt right leaving Jeri alone. Faithfully he waits for me to come and join him each day. There is an irony in it. Bed, a place I longed to be free of for so long, is now my safe space. Jeri and I whisper to each other about the day. Was it good, bad, horrible, or magnificent? How much pain during the day? How much mental and emotional struggle?

The daily pain of neuropathy most often settles down a little when I get under the covers. My hearing aids out, glasses resting in their cases, and my clerical shirt changed for the comfort of pajamas. The night brings solace and escape from the day. And I remember. I remember a bed full of fluid. I remember being iced down to break a threatening fever. I remember cold and shivering abated by a blowup cover that had warm air pumped through it. I recall tubes with bulbs to collect fluids hanging from my sides. The memories of hallucinations, horrible and coruscating, are re-membered in my mind, still real and robust. Jeri knows. No one else can.

Now I carry the burdens of others again. This is always holy ground. Burdens and suffering are sacred. So are scars. Jeri bears his share, as do I. It would be a mistake to want to be rid of it all, an error to think that something truly harrowing and heartbreaking wasn't also divine. Holy is a word that has a different meaning for me now. It has been divorced from puritanical notions and sentiments about human perfectionism. I'm not sure how long I can remain a shepherd, bearing the burdens of others. The path of ministry does take a toll even on the healthiest of bodies and minds, the leading of a church even more so. Demands and expectations, even if they are simply self-expectations, compound over the years.

The promise of anticipation at the beginning of this journey is gone. I no longer expect to be "better." I thought that my life of living with disease would be over with the new organ, but that was exchanged for other, albeit less life-threatening, diseases which are ever-present. I wrestle with who I am, what I should be, and even what to do with the life left to me. Scripture is filled with wisdom that could be applied. Jeri and I listen to the daily lectionary lessons being read from an app. A nice calming voice comes to us with the words of the Bible, just as they did in those last few weeks of our stay at Mount Sinai.

I think about how to live now, to what should attention be given. Love the Lord God with all my mind, soul, heart, strength, and my neighbor as myself. That sticks with me, but there are so many forms that can take. Perhaps it is to seek justice, love mercy, and walk humbly with God. That's another good one, great wisdom to that, but again so many ways to go about it. It turns over and over in my mind without resolution.

How to live in the wake of it all.

Sometimes I do strange things. I need to remember it all. I searched online for the sound of the ventilator system used at Mount Sinai. Of all the sounds I remember, that one evokes the most visceral and powerful response, and yet it is surprisingly comforting. It sends me to the places I was in my many travels from that hospital bed, which was my home for so long. I need to remember and most importantly never minimize or write off what I endured as something less than it was—horrible and unimaginable, yet necessary for healing.

For my friend and I, I can only say that we try to fill our days and to make our days full. But as with most people who look for purpose and full days, there is always a sense of so much waste. It snowed again today. My scars have faded, as have the blood stains that are on Jeri. We are bound, this one and I, by experience and DNA. We agree some days are just to be got through. They are mundane or awful. Other days are cherished: sacred because they brought with them the sacraments of hugs, love, joy, and time with family and close friends.

Epilogue

Jeri and I are believers. We believe in the kindness and generosity of individuals and communities. We believe in people who have dedicated their lives to improving the health and saving the lives of others. We believe in the gift of family and friends. We also want to hope. But hope requires faith, or it is nothing. Sometimes faith itself is hard to find; it is a seed planted by God deep in the soil of each of our hearts. That seed needs nurturing and cultivation. Sometimes it has to be found again because it has been swept away by the trials of life, but it is there, an ember at times, but there, nonetheless.

I remember so well when my wheelchair was being pushed to the door of Mount Sinai Hospital. Jeri and I smelled the air from Madison Avenue coming in, the warmth of a New York July to meet us. All that was in front of us, and we were in shock that it was happening. We still are in shock at times that we survived and that we managed to roll through those doors to the busy New York street, even more so when we transferred into the car, shut the door, and heard only the din of the street. A quiet and a wave of peace overcame us. I wasn't sure my fragile body could make it all the way home, three hours away. No tubes, no IV, no ventilator, no hospital smell or sound. Jeri and I made it out. There next to us was Nancy, happy, rejoicing, and Jeri always with a smile that whispers: "It's going to be okay. I'm here with you. Whatever may come, believe."

Jeri is like that and the better part of me remembers that in many ways we were better then; when we were utterly broken, and had passed through God's fire, pure and refined—a perfect wreck of humanity. In that place, Jeri reminds me that God was indeed closer than we could ever imagine. Believe. Yes, Jeri, I know, is an object, but he is an object sacred to me. He reminds me as well that over and above all the inexplicable suffering and loss there stands a divine shepherd attending and awaiting us. Christianity holds the promise of something, Someone, who is for humanity, for us—*pro nobis* in Latin. God in the midst. God in the storm. God in the pain and anguish. God in the grief. God that is mysteriously rooting for us. God ever and always, even impossibly—*pro nobis*.

Afterword
by Nancy Titus

On the day I called, you answered me,

you increased my strength of soul.

—Psalm 138:3—

People often ask me how I do it. How do I navigate the multiplicity of challenges that come my way? They asked this a lot when Eric was in the hospital, and I was managing a household from afar. My reply was that I was buoyed on the prayers of God's people. No doubt about it, I could not have made it without those constant prayers going up for Eric and me and our family from all over the world. This is Eric's story and while mine runs parallel, it is quite a different one full of many parts I won't detail here. Mine is fundamentally a story of prayer, prayer that started decades before we ever ventured to a hospital in Manhattan, back when we knew a transplant was on some distant horizon in some unknowable future. For all I couldn't possibly know, one thing I did know for sure: I was going to need help to navigate this!

From the first day he entered Mount Sinai Hospital and every day thereafter, I believed Eric would recover, but I also was very aware that he might not. We had talked about the possibility of the transplant not working. He was ready for what that meant. I was too. But naively, we thought the process would be more decisive. Either it would work, or it wouldn't. We never anticipated this long, long, winding road of not-quite working, improving then plummeting downward, only to climb back up and plunge down again. So many hard-won victories only to be put right back on the

Afterword

ventilator and start all over again. Even after the second transplant, he had so many different infections and other complications.

What held me up were the words from the first chapter of First Peter where Jesus is described as giving us a "living hope through the resurrection of Jesus Christ from the dead" (1:3b). I was sure this was the verse for me for this time of trial. It helped me to continue to believe despite what my eyes told me as I looked into a face that died a little more every day. In honestly reading the context of the verse, however, I couldn't be sure that the Lord wasn't preparing me for the ultimate resurrection on the other side of this life, the one that is "imperishable, undefiled, and unfading, kept in heaven" for us (v. 4). I tried to stand firm in faith believing Eric would live while also recognizing the limitations of my understanding and God's sovereignty over when he would die. The concept of a *living hope* would not leave me, however. It connected me with something transcendent. My sister sent me a care package which included a bracelet with an anchor on it. I wore it every day, and every day that little anchor token got caught repeatedly on my clothing, as a little enactment of this verse with a hope not of my creation that would not stop digging itself in, making itself noticed, and anchoring me to the possibility of life beyond what I could see.

For a little more than four months, from October 28, 2019, until March 6, 2020, I lived in Manhattan at Mount Sinai's Transplant Living Center. I stayed as much as possible by my husband's side, only occasionally rushing back home to grab the mail, check in with our congregation, maybe do laundry, and touch base with a family that was in many ways losing its bearings. The days were long and lonely and filled with uncertainty. I spent hours and hours and hours mostly sitting in a chair beside his bed, trying to stay on top of what was happening to him, trying to keep all our praying friends abreast of the latest details. I am an optimistic person because I believe in a powerful God, and I knew the prayers were keeping us going.

As it unfolded, day after day, I looked in the face of death and was challenged to believe anyway. I could see what Eric could not, what he later was shocked to find when he finally had a look in the mirror. I could see he was losing the battle, and yes, in some of it—the eating—I felt he had given up too soon, thus the painful food fights. One of my lowest points was a heart-wrenching shopping trip I had at the grocery store just before Christmas, when I was buying baby food to take back to him to coax a little more nutrition into him in as gentle a way as possible. At the store where I worked, I prayed that no one would notice me because I knew I

Afterword

would break down right there in the aisle if even one person asked about him and showed even the slightest bit of compassion. I went home and prepared some special dishes for Christmas, some of his favorites, blended so he wouldn't gag. He barely even tried to eat two bites. That problem evaporated, though, in the crisis that followed, when he went into the coma on December 30, and eating didn't become a possibility for him again until June.

God brought people to me that helped me hold on. Of course, people I already knew were providing all manner of support from a distance, and now new ones were added up close. I went to the nearest church from our denomination, Elmendorf Reformed Church, the oldest church in Harlem. The pastor and people there enfolded me in their embrace and lifted me in prayer. Because one Sunday they had no service, I searched for another. Valerie was with me when I told her the name: Church of the Living Hope. How could I not go there? This small group of believers also kept me going, especially after the Covid shutdown as I was able to worship virtually with those in closer proximity to Eric, people who were themselves living in the shadow of a disease that was taking their loved ones.

Besides all the transplant drama at Mount Sinai, life was also going on back at our home in Red Hook, roughly one hundred miles north of Manhattan, a two-to-three hour drive up the Taconic State Parkway. Some of it was normal, and some were crises all their own. As weeks faded into months, though, everything changed. When Eric entered Mount Sinai, we were living in a large parsonage next to the church he pastored, a family of seven: Eric, me, our son, Samuel and, Jack, his spouse, daughters, Valerie and Penelope, and Eric's mother, Connie. By the time of his second transplant, ninety days later, there was only one person "living" in that large house: Penelope, our youngest. Samuel and Jack moved to Michigan, a plan that had been in place for months before the surgery. Valerie moved in with friends back at her old college in Georgia. Grandma moved into a nursing home. Even our dog moved out.

Penelope turned 20 in December, the same day that Grandma had surgery on a broken wrist suffered in a fall the week before. Though technically an adult, it was too much for Penelope to stay in the house alone during that emotionally fraught time, and she sought refuge with various church members and even flew to be with Valerie in Savannah for a time. I came back home to be with her and to pick up other pieces of our lives. I planned to reverse my split life by staying at home, returning to work in

Afterword

a grocery store pharmacy, and commuting two to three times a week to Manhattan to see Eric. I started riding the train, which saved a little wear and tear on me but still required me to drive for an hour to get to the station in Poughkeepsie, ride the train for ninety minutes, and then walk half an hour from the station to the hospital and then do it all in reverse later in the day. Every day of my commute, there were fewer and fewer people on the train, as Covid began its rampage across New York.

Unfortunately, just as my visits were becoming fewer, Eric was becoming more disconnected from reality. He described walking by a mirror and seeing a knife wound on his back, no doubt referring to a very real and large bed sore that was causing havoc with his tender skin. He thought what he experienced was real, but I was there in the step-down unit beside him, watching his legs thrash about under the sheets as he slept. I reminded him that a couple hours earlier it had taken two physical therapists to help him just to transfer from the bed to the chair next to it, that he couldn't possibly stand on his own, much less walk across a room. He only partially understood my logic. He shared other things with me, and I could tell that he needed me to help him discern between his delusional or hallucinogenic dream-state and reality. I only saw him a couple more times before they shut the hospital down to visitors due to Covid. Despite my pleas about his deteriorating mental state, I was not allowed to see him, to be an anchor for him. We would be separated for ten agonizing weeks. In addition, five days after they shut the hospital down, he was moved back to the Transplant Intensive Care Unit and placed back on the ventilator.

During those ten weeks, Eric would be shuffled to many different floors as the hospital staff worked desperately to contain the Covid threat that had taken over everything. First, I was told the entire Transplant Intensive Care Unit had been moved to what is normally a surgical recovery area to give its former space to critical Covid patients. Other times my call would be shuffled from one unit to another before his new location was made known. Every time, I would have to wait fifteen minutes or more while his nurse was located only to be told he was about the same as nurses were limited in the medical information they could provide. It was a frustrating time of not really knowing what was happening, having to trust that no news was good news.

Worst of all is that he was unable to communicate with me in any way. Before I left him, he was unable to hold a pen. He couldn't hold his phone. On the ventilator, he couldn't talk. He could not even ask a nurse to call me

Afterword

for him. On the rare occasions that the overworked nurses could make a video call for him, he would ask why I wouldn't go see him. How could he possibly understand what the pandemic had done to all of us? The day I finally got a text from him, while I was working at the pharmacy, was such a joy! He was learning to use his phone again. I would barrage him with texts. He would write a line or two days later. But at least some connection, finally!

Then the devastating blow that he tested positive for Covid and was further isolated. He was still in a Covid unit when I was finally allowed to go see him on May 25. I had to don all the protective equipment: gown, mask, gloves. But he could see some of my face and I could see his! I could touch him through gloved hands, not ideal but a real connection, at last!

It was a joyous day when I brought him home. But the journey was not over. It would be months yet before he could do many normal things. My brother died and I was unable to go to the funeral in Texas: Eric couldn't travel, and I couldn't leave him. We had a dear friend and missionary colleague who was fighting a terminal battle with cancer. We desperately wanted to see her and her husband, who was on dialysis and needed a kidney transplant. We drove to see them just as soon as Eric recovered enough for us to make that long drive to Wisconsin, just weeks before our friend passed. We were able to stop on the way home for a belated anniversary and celebration of his survival at an iconic Michigan inn where Eric's grandparents had spent their honeymoon.

Since then, I have seen Eric rebound in incredible ways. Despite his many continued physical struggles, including considerable pain and neuropathy, he leads a congregation. He serves faithfully, though thankfully at a considerably slower pace than before. He laments that he is different, that he has lost some of the mental sharpness that once was his pride and joy. I encourage him that many of the differences add up to him being kinder and gentler, mostly to himself and then to me as he has always dealt well with those under his ministerial care. It is as if some of the sharper edges have been smoothed over in this purifying process he has endured. He clearly misses his sharper self, though. This, too, I understand. But I am so proud of him, this private man I married who never wanted to share any of his personal medical information who has written a book detailing it in all its tremendous vulnerability. It's a wonder, really, and not something that other, more self-assured man would have done. He has brought us spiritual insights gleaned from those difficult days and unending nights in the house

Afterword

of pain. I give thanks for the indomitable spirit of my beloved who came back to us from that far country and has graced us with hard-won wisdom gleaned there.

I cry as I remember that time and the hardships we all endured, but I rejoice in the triumph of it. I acknowledge with humility the many, many people along the way who assisted us in our journey and made the unthinkable palatable. But most of all, I am thankful for God who heard my years of crying out about this eventuality and met me in it. It was from a source not my own that I was able to respond with conviction on December 31 when the critical care doctor gave me the updates of Eric's infections and their efforts to thwart them. When he said "but we're only human," designed I know to prepare me for a death that seemed so likely at the time, something *inside* me but not *of* me burst forth with the response: "That's OK. We've got the rest covered!" Because I knew God had.

Even as we would walk a tight-rope for another month, watching human hope fade as the window of opportunity for a second transplant narrowed with the ticking clock, this living hope of a resurrected Jesus would not give up on me or on Eric. Even after he survived that surgery and a continual onslaught of various infections afterward, this living hope kept us going. When I had to walk away and could not return to my bedside post for weeks, this living hope worked in both of us, resurrected itself in one of us, and miraculously brought us back together for a purpose God knows. To God be the glory! Amen.

Appendix
Death and Dying

The boundaries which divide Life from Death are at best shadowy and vague. Who shall say where the one ends, and where the other begins?

—Edgar Allen Poe—

The theologian Eberhard Jüngel, in his *Death: The Riddle and Mystery*, maintains that there is no one to whom we as humans may turn and ask the question, "What is death?"[1] Because no one who is living has died and those who are dead cannot speak to the living. Jüngel, whom I very much admire, has, however, discounted to the point of simply ignoring the phenomenon of near-death experiences. While I would generally agree with Jüngel's statement, I must respond with a dialectical Yes and No. As I mentioned elsewhere in this work, I do believe the term near-death experience is a good way of naming the phenomenon. So I, too, would say that near-death is just that, near but not quite.

People like me who have had experiences like this both do and do not have an experience of death. Certainly, as Jüngel points out, there are those who are dying but they are not dead. Certainly, anyone who has had a near-death experience has also had the aspect of dying attached to it. But near-death experiences do provide us with something important. Near-death experiences are like touching or tasting death, without completely severing ties to the present reality. Michael Grosso bears this out in his 1981 article in *Anabiosis: The Journal for Near-Death Studies*. There

---

1. Eberhard Jüngel, *Death: The Riddle and the Mystery* (Philadelphia: Westminster, 1974), 3.

are also psychodynamic elements present in near-death experiences, but as Bruce Greyson points out in response to Grosso's article: "We do not know enough about [near-death experiences] yet to formulate comprehensive models, and it may be that when we do know more about these phenomena, we will discover that certain elements are not reducible to psychological constructs."[2] I can only respond to this with "correct."

There were in my near-death experiences elements that I can identify as psychological, things I know that were perhaps influenced by my faith and identity. But here the construct ends. My near-death experiences were often religious, but not completely corresponding to my faith and yet not alien to it. I have read a few flamboyant books regarding Christians who have had near-death experiences. Often these accounts, however, run afoul for me in that they are usually verbatim depictions of the person's understanding of angels and such. Whatever the experience here, which may simply be a delusion or hallucination, it is never beyond the mental construct of the person. Near-death experiences tend to be more than, other than, while not being in contradiction to a particular faith system. It is difficult to state. However, from a Christian standpoint, if God is truly transcendent and wholly other, that means that God is completely different from me, or anyone else for that matter. The prophet Isaiah states the case well when speaking for God: "For my thoughts are not your thoughts, nor are your ways my ways" (Isa 55:8).

I think that Christians run quickly to these accounts and are taken in by them for a singular reason: they yearn for verification of their faith. It is why they want the shroud of Turin to be the real burial cloth of Jesus or why they want to find the Ark of Noah or the Ark of the Covenant. It's also why I believe many Christians are star-struck by celebrity. If such a famous person believes, why then the claims of Christianity must be true! But for me the danger here is a matter of faith, that is, what is faith put in? Is my faith in the shroud of Turin? Is it in Noah's Ark? Is it in the testimony of a person that had a near-death experience and saw Jesus? Is my faith in the faith of the latest superstar to convert? My faith is in none of those things. My faith in is Christ alone. It resides there, unfailing, stalwart. Did I see Jesus? No. Neither did I see a bright white light at the end of a tunnel. What

---

2. Bruce Greyson, "Toward a Psychological Explanation of Near-Death Experiences: A Response to Dr. Grosso's Paper," *Anabiosis: The Journal for Near-Death Studies* 1/2 (1981): 88.

Appendix

I did experience, see, touch, smell, hear, was a world beyond me. The past, present, future—where temporal time conceded to eternity.

Jüngel's primary goal in his little but dense book is to forward a Christian theology of death, and he does a marvelous job of this. But, the mystery remains, what is it actually like to die? And this is where I must affirm Jüngel's proposition that we simply cannot know for certain what that answer is. This is for two reasons. The first I have already stated. The second is a problem of experience that cannot be met with adequate language. A person experiencing a true near-death experience (and not a construction of hallucination) will lack the language necessary to convey the most critical information needed. Perhaps that is by design.

By way of example, I offer the following. I became conscious to find I was in a thick narrow passage. It was soft, yet firm, foam-like, and green if I remember correctly. I began hearing voices. I was trying to communicate with people. Unable to speak, I had to convey my thoughts in powerful non-verbal, non-physical ways. I managed to do this, still surrounded by the thickness. Then I tried to press through it. However, I paused when I heard voices calling from another direction, another passage less narrow, and easier to navigate. Now voices in two different places calling me to them. Which to choose? Perhaps the narrow passage was harder, but my theology also teaches that the way to the kingdom of God is narrow. Try the narrow? I did, but eventually I could push ahead no further, almost like I was in a birth canal. Then I heard the voices the other way, the way I eventually went.

It was a dimensionally felt sense experience. It sounds mundane on paper, but it was trans-mundane in experience. This was a part of one of my near-death experiences. I wonder where I would be now if I had pressed through the narrower passageway. Was the will and need of this present age greater and more pressing than the patient kingdom of the eternal divine one? I think of this, and I recall Jesus saying, "For the gate is narrow and the road is hard that leads to life, and there are few who find it" (Matt 7:14). It probably had nothing to do with my near-death experience, but it is a curious synchronicity.

There is another thing I can relate about my near-death experiences. In many such accounts, there is what is termed a "review of life." In Christian theology, this would be something like the judgment seat of Christ. In many cases, these are instantaneous, like their life passing before their eyes. This instantaneous review didn't happen to me. Rather, they came as

Appendix

slow encounters with the past interwoven in a new world, each of which I had to come to terms with. And there was something else that happened: adventure, sometimes fantastical, sometimes more peaceful, and in a great many cases frightful. Sometimes I also knew I was still tied to my bed, and yet I was trying to break free. I was perhaps, in this way, trying to escape dying, to meet death and whatever it held fully.

Many people have asked me during my career as a minister whether I was afraid of death. I always said no. I felt that the theology that supported my faith was reasonable and sound. I still feel this way. My reply also was that I was more afraid of the dying process, the pain it might involve, and the suffering that might come in body and mind. I was afraid of a long process of dying before reaching death. I can now say I was right to be afraid of that! A lingering process was mine. A hellish dying process met me with all the fear and force I could have conjured in my imagination. I have done dying to death I suppose. So, yes, I still fear that. That might meet me again before death overtakes me. I don't live in dread of it. I guess like I feel like I already paid that part of it, so perhaps God will be merciful to me and give me time served when I die. On occasion I've seen people die peacefully and in their sleep. This is the preferred way of dying, I've found, in talking with people during my ministry. It's surely how I'd like to die.

As for what is "on the other side of death," I must say we simply don't know what the other side might bring. I know, Christians everywhere right now are throwing their hands up and invoking all sorts of invectives against me: *non-believer*, *O ye of little faith*, even *heretic*. It perhaps also might be met with cocksureness, ignorance, and arrogance. So be it. I simply am relaying my experience and trying to reconcile it to my theology, if possible. We do believe that judgment follows death. Judgment is often referred to as the day of judgment. But of course, if we read Scripture synchronically, a day for God is as a thousand years for us, as the Apostle Peter writes. Time, I have learned, is both a concrete phenomenon based on measurable movements of planets *and* an arbitrary transmundane phenomenon that lacks concreteness by our standards. Death itself then, taking into consideration its complete "otherness" from all our vast variety of human earthly experience, simply by its unknowingness, does make me a bit more reluctant to say that I'm not somewhere in the corner of my mind terrified of the prospect. I think to be otherwise is human hubris.

After what I've been through I "get" the idea of "fear of the Lord." I think it's natural, in fact. Not that I abandon the mercy or the constituent

Appendix

nature of God as love. I affirm these too from my study, my earthly experience, and yes from my near-death experiences. To be in the presence of a being that is totally other and to somehow confuse my human understanding of love with a divine being that *is* love and not to feel trepidation is to jump into a categorical confusion of the worst sort. God is righteousness and holiness, too. Based on those same things I can also say, we will give answer. It seems that we live to reflect those things, as my dear late friend and colleague Corneliu Constantineanu points out in his book Επαγγελια: *An Exegetical Study of the Concept of Promise in the Pauline Corpus*: "There is a kind of tension between God's given promises and the implied conditions that the recipients of the promises should fulfill in a certain way."[3] How we live in this life matters in the next. Of this, I am now convinced. I am more circumspect about who I am, the faith I hold, *and* how I conduct myself according to this faith. This is in part, I think, because I have retrospectively formulated an idea that God holds us to the faith standard we adopt. I know this is a problematic thing to say, but then again, hypocrisy and hypocrites were something of a theme that Jesus concerned himself with and called others on.

Don't get me wrong. I don't live my days in dread and fear. Quite the opposite. I look back on this with awe and wonder at the marvel of it all. I long at some level to be there again. Mind you, I love life. I have loved my life with all its ups and downs, joys and sorrows. I have packed a great deal of living into my life. I love my life. And I am convinced beyond persuasion that death is not the end of us (and as a theologian I have had serious doubts, I must confess). As the Swiss Reformed theologian Karl Barth stated in his *Time* magazine interview in April 1962, "The goal of human life is not death, but resurrection." I approach death with a blend of excited anticipation and a healthy fear of the unknown.

It also hasn't escaped me that the afterlife may be different things to different people. Even within my Christian tradition, we juggle terminology and eschatology, a part of theology that deals with all things related to "the end," including death. At the foundation of our faith there exists the Judaic concept of *Sheol*. Then there is *paradise, heaven, hell, Gehenna, the new heaven and new earth*. Frankly, these are terms that are employed to speak of the afterlife without getting into details about the afterlife we simply don't have. They are words that attempt to point to something to which

---

3. Corneliu Constantineanu, *Επαγγελια: An Exegetical Study of the Concept of Promise in the Pauline Corpus* (Osijek: ETF, 2005), 41.

we wish to give conceptuality. These are the foundations of our reflections on the afterlife. However, I must say I am dismayed about how Christians approach eschatology. I am not opining here about some of the more fanciful eschatologies that Hal Lindsay or the *Left Behind* series have ground into the popular imagination. I'm talking about hard-core academics and scholars. One of the best treatments of eschatology, other than Moltmann's beautiful *Theology of Hope* and thought-provoking *The Coming of God*, is Hans Schwarz's *Eschatology*. It is a marvelous work covering the entire topic. He dedicates six pages to the topic of near-death experiences. I must give Schwarz credit, since he interacts, albeit briefly, with some of the chief scholars in near-death experience studies such as Raymond Moody, Kenneth Ring, Carol Zaleski, and Bruce Greyson along with others. However, I would dispute that near-death experiences are limited to those pronounced "clinically dead."

One of the more serious near-death experience memoirs is from Eben Alexander, a neurosurgeon. Alexander had a very rare neurological disease and fell into a coma. He was not pronounced clinically dead. Yet, he had many of the same types of experiences that I had, and that others have had who have experienced a near-death. Being pronounced "clinically dead" may happen. It also may not, and this is a part of the mystery. While Schwarz names and deals with this important component of eschatology, it is not expansive enough. Still, he bravely wades into waters where many would yell "That's all of the devil." But it is not.

As Christians we deal in great part with death, and what the afterlife is. Yet, we have academically really shunned the psychological and parapsychological because of trepidation of two things: a reviling of those who might condemn us for asking and seeking legitimate answers to the question of the afterlife on the one hand and perhaps being associated with what some may view as more "dubious" academic disciplines. Parapsychology is often associated with ridiculous "ghost-hunter" shows and seances, but there are true academics in this field trying to find these answers, too. The Koestler Institute at the University of Edinburg is an example of this, but there are many others as well. It seems to me that Christians tend to build sometimes wild, sometimes more sound, conclusions about matters of the afterlife strictly from Scripture. I would agree that Scripture should inform theology. The problem is that Scripture is largely silent about this matter. We are given snippets, metaphors, and pictures. For Christians what must stand as the result is the concept of resurrection, also a difficult matter to understand. But the question: *What exactly happens when we die?* is still an open question to which at best we shrug our shoulders. A simple "we go to be with the Lord" is less than satisfying.

Christian theology I think needs to be bold and step into the discussion with psychologists and parapsychologists who pursue these questions with academic earnestness. Frankly, we have nothing to lose. We may stigmatize these sorts of investigations (again I'm not talking Ghostbusters here), or perhaps we can wade in with these scholars and find illumination for our understanding of Scripture. Perhaps a deeper understanding of our uniqueness might be forthcoming, and perhaps our theological discipline might inform them. I don't think we lose a great deal by entering an honest discussion about these matters. Perhaps this is being done. I haven't done enough investigation into the matter to know. Some might say that I should do it since I feel like I've had a near-death experience. However, my attention is focused first on other issues in Christianity, and foremost, I lack the one thing that I would need above all else in doing so—objectivity.

As a Christian, who experienced what I believe to have been near-death experiences, I believed and now I more firmly believe in the death of death. Christian theology in the resurrection of Jesus Christ maintains, as the bedrock of its faith, that death has been defeated and overcome, and further that this event echoes both to the past and into the future. "Christ has triumphed o'er the grave" as the Christmas hymn "Hark! the Herald Angels Sing" goes. In Christ's triumph, we have also triumphed. This is at the core of Christianity.

www.ingramcontent.com/pod-product-compliance
Lightning Source LLC
Chambersburg PA
CBHW070455090426
42735CB00012B/2557